O SHEPHERD, WHERE ART THOU?

O SHEPHERD, WHERE ART THOU?

Calvin Miller

BROADMAN
& HOLMAN
PUBLISHERS

Nashville, Tennesee

13-digit ISBN: 978-0-8054-4098-0
10-digit ISBN: 0-8054-4098-4

Published by Broadman & Holman Publishers,
Nashville, Tennessee

Dewey Decimal Classification: 253
Subject Heading: PASTORAL CARE

10 09 08 07 06   1 2 3 4 5 6 7 8 9 10 11 12 13 14 15

Contents

v

Chapter One

I'm a new man!" Sam exulted as he parked his golf cart just to the side of the first tee. "I love being alive!" He set his golf bag down and smiled as he shoved a tee into the sod. "And just to think, this used to be my hospital day. No more! I'm free!" The soft earth oozed a dewy welcome as it yielded to his tee. The whole world was about to yield to his tee. Sam felt it all the way down to his two-toned shoes. His newly improved golf swing was only the outward sign of a new anointing.

And who had brought about this change?

Will Willington, pastor of Newark's Park Brook Community Church, that's who!

And of course the Holy Spirit, working through Will's life. But it never occurred to Sam to think of the Holy Spirit and Will Willington at the same time. The Holy Spirit was way back in the Bible, and Will Willington was in the "real" world of heaven and hype. The world of what's happening now!

Willington had attracted more than fifty thousand adherents. But they more than adhered; they adored, they admired and admonished all who would not admit to Willington's greatness. The pastor of Newark's prestigious Park Brook Community Church and author of *Physician, Heal Thyself, How to Kiss Pastoral Care Good-bye Forever.* What a book! Because of that book Sam had finally come to see the light. He found a way to be free of ministry and still get ministry done. Sam had known for years his church

1

*Structuring for growth is the one essential that says that growth never happens unless we plan for it to happen. Praying for it to happen and hoping it will may result in the pastor being godly or optimistic, but the real result of church growth always happens because the church structures for it. Bob Sorrell suggests that this planning is most effective when the pastor includes the church in the plan.

Form a planning team with a good cross section of gifted and mature people, those with wisdom and discernment—men and women, young and old—and be sure they are not all just like you. Some need to be people who "color outside the box," and some need to be those who specialize in creating artistry inside the box. Depending on the size of the church, your team may be as few as three people for a bivocational church, and as many as seven for larger churches. . . . Be wise about the people you include. Invite mature people of varied orientations to join the process so you will avoid "group think." Some people, such as the pastoral staff and lay leadership, need to be an integral part of the entire process.[1]

†What causes plateau in church life is "interiorization." Erwin McManus writes, "For some churches, maintaining a standard of hymns and pews has been more important than changing the world around them. Now, we have to live with the reality that, all too many times, we kept our traditions and lost our children. For others the real issue became the tension between relevance and revolution. We became the masters of programming and strangely enough, knowledge of the Bible. The focus deteriorated to formatting around the desires of Christians." Once the church focuses on itself, plateau is on the way.[2]

wasn't growing, but he never knew why until the dynamic Will Willington collided with his lackluster life. Before Will—B. W.— he had been so wrapped up in his ministry to the sick and dying he didn't have time to grow a church. Now he knew the truth: churches don't grow because they will not structure for growth.* Will Willington had made that clear.

Most pastors live forever in the barren wasteland of pastoral care because they just don't structure for growth. Will Willington understood this. And why wouldn't he? He was no longer merely a pastor. He was the 007 of the needy church growth world. He was leading the dying-church Exodus out of the captivity of their postdenominational Egypts. Oh how Will hated failure, and plateaued churches were just that.† While Will never ate manna himself, he served it to the lesser ones, the counted ones, those who had settled down in Sinai. Sure, some of them thoughtlessly got sick, usually after they joined the church. It was so devious of them—they'd join the church all smiling and healthy, then boom! Into the hospital they went, calling for the church to come see them. But now he had written the book—he had written several books, actually—on how things were to be done.

Sam long ago had read his first book, *Zones of Compassion*. It was all about how minipastors could become mega if they would free themselves of their poor self-image by dividing their church fields into the zones where their congregations lived. This was the basis of his zone theory of pastoral care. It was all explained in the chapter "Zonify or Die." So Sam had already divided his congregation into zones. He had appointed care committees of compassion to handle all the sick or psychologically needy in their zones of compassion. Then the care committees would allow the pastors to become "preaching pastors" with a shot at a real reputation. Once pastors had "zonified" themselves free of the need to

*Does God intend for every church to get bigger? And is the only way to get bigger to have more members? I always counsel my students to make sure they are making bigger people and not just bigger congregations. There are many pastors serving in areas where the population density is too small and static to support a growing congregation. Are these servants to live under the pall of inferiority just because their churches are not getting bigger? I think not.

"We need to rethink what successful ministry is all about," said Mark Stephenson. "While most of us hear only about the success of the mega-church, there are successes in small church ministry that we never hear about. The success stories that we hear almost always come from mega-churches, because small churches don't get much respect in a culture that values 'supersize.'"[3]

†How we see ourselves is probably the result of seeing what God has called us to do. Christopher Laasch wrote in the 1980s of our devotion to narcissism. Sociologists for the most part agree that we left that stage with the eighties. Still it seems to me that most successful churches have kept alive in their own minds the narrow culture of egotism. Often it seems to me that large churches do what they encourage small churches not to do: to worship themselves. The packaging of success is sometimes the wrappings of a light and frothy happiness. In fact, Marva Dawn has warned us away form this idolatry of happiness. Self-esteem, based on an honest understanding of our individuality and our God-called place in the kingdom, is the healthiest of all mystiques. It keeps our worship centered on God and not any other heroes—megachurch pastors, notwithstanding—and gives us a healthy appraisal, who we are apart from the numbers of the church growth mentality.[4]

‡Marva Dawn realizes how futile it is to try to trump up a vital self-image by pasting together the best part of those heroes we might wish to worship. It struck me one day in a Christian bookstore that most of the "church growth" books I picked up in that store were not books on vision but on image. They hadn't been published to help me see the world in a particular way but to help the world see me—were I a megachurch pastor—in a particular way. They were books that enticed the pastor of limited self-image to be like somebody else the world admired. What a cul-de-sac of emotional poverty this is. These books were published to serve the idolatries of megapastor wannabes. Marva Dawn writes, "Because our relationship with God frees us from having to justify our own existence, we do not have to prove our importance, fit in with our peers, mimic the politically correct, or think according to the current ideologies and idolatries. Our minds are captive only to Christ's lordship; the Holy Spirit empowers us to use the brains God created as well as possible."[5]

minister to their congregations, they could devote their time to getting bigger just like God intended.*

On the very morning after Sam had finished reading Will's second book, *You Too Can Be a Megaman of God,* Sam found himself golfing. He was golfing solo, but his game had never been better. He had found a new direction for his life; why wouldn't his golf be better? His life was.

He was close to delirious with his new self-image. *You Too Can Be a Megaman of God* was only 103 pages (with very wide margins and huge print), but it was the *magnum opus* of Will Willington, megapastor. Who knew how large Will's church really was? Forty thousand? Some said it was eighty thousand. But Pastor Will himself usually told others that it was fifty thousand, although he liked reminding his admirers that fifty thousand was in reality one-twentieth of a million. Even as he watched the Park Brook videos, Sam could not help thinking, *The gods have come down in the likeness of men.* Sam was a small fry, but as Will had said, "You're only a 'small fry' 'cause you fry small."†

It was not a brilliant proverb, but it had helped Sam to see that he needed a bigger fryer if he was going to fry bigger. And as Willington had said, Colonel Sanders had conquered the world with a bigger fryer. The point was that Sam felt good about himself as he began his Monday morning game of golf. The sick had care. His church could grow. He, too, could be a big man.‡

"This one's for you, Will," he said as he squared his shoulders, raked the shank of the chrome and graphite club past his shoulders. "Mega, mega, mega!" he shouted as he brought the blitzkrieg club swinging its rotary fire past his thigh—even as the poor ball begged him to hold his blazing club. The ball was powerless. It clicked the head of the club. Poor thing! It had no choice but to fly. Megaman Sam held the club. "Oh, I am good!" cried Willington's

*Sam's desire to mega seems to overlook the great truth. The average size church in America is small and getting smaller. In 1997 the average church in America had 102 in attendance each Sunday. But only a year later, this had dropped to 91. This alarming short-term drop in attendance was accompanied by a similar drop of 15 percent in the operating budgets of those same churches.[6]

man. Sam smiled as his shot flew like a bullet through the blue ether of morning, straight down the fairway! He was free.

Even as his ball soared he knew that someday his church budget would be printed on bond. *Oh, hasten the day. Even so come, Lord Jesus, but not till I've succeeded,* thought Sam. *Hold the trumpet, Gabe, until the Salary category of my budget has many names under mine that all begin with the word "Associate."* Sam knew that when that happened all those salaries would have to be lumped under one category. Then the world would tremble. He would have his own church credit card. And no one—not even the nosiest of deacons—would have an inkling of how much he made. Did everybody know what Will Willington made? Of course not! Only God and the IRS knew, and the IRS wasn't completely sure.

He swung once more. His golf was impeccable. He couldn't hook. Slicing was impossible. He was golfing in Zion. There was no sickness anywhere in his parish for which he was responsible. Par was his middle name. Hole after hole, his sweet little dimpled ball kissed its way—birdielike—into the cup. His golf, his self-image, his entire world was "mega." Soon his church would be.*

But what would he name his church? Something with *Brook* in the title, of course. All megachurches had *brook* or *creek* or *river* in the title. And where would he relocate it? Beyond the beltway on eighty acres of rolling wonderland, just like Will Willington. Of course, he would have to wait until the time was right to tell the lesser people what the name would be. But he would pick out the name now so he would be all ready to do it when the time came.

Suddenly he froze. He couldn't call it something with the words *brook* and *creek* in the title. He couldn't. Blast it all! There wasn't a brook of any kind anywhere near his church. There was a little rill behind his church. It was dry most of the year, but after a very heavy rain there was some water in it, which emptied into

*Sam's deliberation of what to name his megachurch is reflective of a new "flatness" in architecture. Perhaps the flatness comes from a "flat" view of what the church exists to do. Evangelicals have long been one dimensional as to the purpose of the church. The church existed to win souls, and to get it all done fast, before Jesus came again. Hence the shape of our buildings and the names of our churches reflect our one-dimensional urgency. No one would ever decry the importance of evangelism, but the simplicity of our urgency has left us unhooked to any *great* traditions or urgency. Os Guinness says that we have adopted a marketing style. "Style, style, style—style is a leading currency in modern society; the river of life for American consumerism, the main artery of American identity and belonging."

Under the crush of this pressure, megachurches have often opted for noncontent names. The names of the churches rarely reflect the heroes and martyrs of the faith. Instead they tend to be named after neighborhoods or streets or directions. They have a lot of style but often not much substance. Os Guinness reminds us that style and substance often vary inversely. But most condemning is the idea that "every style is the outer expression of the inner character of the period." The only megachurch I have visited that seems to have led the culture rather than mimicked it is Wooddale Church in Minneapolis. Here the name may be culturally generic, but the architecture is thrilling.[7]

†As long as we can cry, "Me!" our lives and callings have no real purpose. This begins when we cry, "His!" Abraham Kuyper wrote, "There is not one square inch of me that does not cry out, 'This is mine! This belongs to me!'" Kierkegaard wrote in his journal, "The thing is to understand myself, to see what God really wants me to do; the thing is to find a truth which is true for me, to find the idea for which I can live and die."[8]

Mimicry has never been a shred of the authentic call. As long as we are possessed by someone else's success, we have not sat long with the Spirit.

Rumpton reservoir. So, right there between the eighth and ninth hole, he made a decision to rename his old church, Rumpton Rill Community Church. Was it right? Was that a good title or what?*
Swing, slam, fire! Right down the fairway! Oh, his golf was good.

He felt like Will Willington was right inside his skin. It was like he was an incarnation of the god of church growth. *Putt, putt,* he thought as he putted the little ball into the cup. It was hopeless; it had to obey him. "Putt, putt!" he said as he putted the ball right up to the edge of the cup. Plop! A perfect putt. As he stooped to pick the ball out of the cup, he smiled and said half aloud. "NO! It is no longer *putt, putt*; it's *vroom, vroom with a sonic boom.* Look out minichurch, megaSam is on the way." He looked around to see if anyone had noticed him talking to himself. There was no one, so he said it again, only louder, "Vroom, vroom!"

It was all so genius. "Mega, mega, mega!" cried Sam, nearly singing. "What a prefix, mega! Oh Lord, I thank you that the first two letters of the word *mega* spell *me.* I never noticed this before. In fact, half of the word *mega* is *me.*† This is clearly a divine revelation. That's been my problem here at church. I've been too humble; it's time I put a little more 'me' in the 'mega.'"
He was through talking to himself for the moment, but only for the moment. He knew Will Willington also played a lot of golf. Now he knew why. Willington was the one man who had never been afraid of putting the 'me' back in 'mega.'

Suddenly Sam's elation fell flat.

Would "zonify or die" really work?

He remembered that there were sick people in his congregation he had promised to visit. He swung his club. Slice, slice, slice, right into the slough. He'd never find the ball. Should he count the stroke? He was playing alone. Who would know? What would Will Willington do? He didn't count the stroke.

*The thing Sam so resented must be for every pastor a moment of resentment. Sickness and death are never considerate of the pastor's schedule. But if we pay the sick no mind, we have already admitted we are only rhetoricians who love speaking the truth but not acting it out. One megapastor of my acquaintance "never makes hospital calls." I find myself not sorry for the sick he ignores, for they are more blessed than he. They are learning the hard lessons of life and the joy that comes from the Savior who is their essential companion. He, on the other hand, is merely writing sermons, of which there is no shortage these days. Further, he is writing and preaching within a sterile atmosphere of his own creation. The country priest said, "Hell is not to love anyone anymore."[9] Of course, not to visit the sick is not to say we are totally unloving. But it may say that to the sick who wait on us and need our special relationship with God (as they see it). Those who suffer while we don't show up are probably thinking with the attitude of the Bard who said, "They do not love who do not show their love."[10]

†A recent book, coauthored by two of America's "most exciting super-church pastors," made virtually no inclusion for pastoral care. They did include ministering to their churches in terms of sports and other kinds of involvement that build community, but ministering to the sick or dying received no significant space in their book. Both churches tend to minister to younger families where dying and sickness are not as frequent as they might be in older fellowships. Says one of these pastors, "We found that one of the most important things to do when trying to create a relevant environment for children is to learn from the experts. Instead of asking other churches what they were doing for their kids, we took our cue from organizations like Nickelodeon and Disney. Over the course of forty-five minutes, we use storytelling, skits, videos, activities, and music designed to both entertain and teach families. A creative team meets each week to plan the twelve segments that make up a typical production. We also have a Web site (www.kidstuf.com) where families can participate and respond to various KidStuf issues."[11]

He golfed on, but none too well. He suddenly had negative thoughts. Willington had warned against negative thinking. Sam felt ashamed. Still the doubt persisted. Between Sam and his post-denominational self-image lay the issue of sick people. He would be expected to visit them, and that would distract him from his megagoals. Why did people have to get sick?* It was so pointless. It kept them from feeling good, and it kept pastors from working on their church growth plans. Sam made himself smile. "I will not be glum. To be glum is dumb," page 75 of *Zones of Compassion,* in a brilliant chapter called "Sick of the Sick? Give It a Flick!" Sam laughed out loud! He had zonified. Yes, sick people had to be cared for, but his sick people were all in zones of compassion. He had already formed his church's zonal care committee.† They were going to do all of Sam's visitation in the future.

No, he didn't have to visit the sick. There were "lesser people" who could do that. Thank the good Lord, there were "the lesser people"! The lesser ones are the ones you count on, page 75 of *You Too Can Be a Megaman of God.* In the world of true church growth there were only a few names; everybody else was a number. *Let the lesser people take care of the lesser people,* Will Willington had said on page 76. Sam thought of it as the spirit of 76. It was his paraphrase of Matthew 8:22.

Just who was it who threatened to wreck his megadreams by getting sick?

Sam thought of Esther Thompson. She had just gone through another operation. Sam would never feel bad about not visiting her. Surgery was her passion. She had more stitching than a Notre Dame football. She loved having things taken out. She had once volunteered to be an organ donor, but she was turned down because she had nothing left to donate. She had gotten sick, but did Sam have to visit her? Noooo! She lived smack dab in the middle of Zone 3.

11

*Sam is obviously counting on solving all his problems by mimicking someone else's programs. "Christian leaders often look at the condition of their churches and attempt to make improvements by applying principles and plans that work well for other churches but not necessarily their own. Wise leaders pattern their plans for the church after God's unique plans and agenda—'God's thumbprint'—for that congregation."[12]

†Most of the reported success stories are blinding us to the true fact of the exact state of Christianity—particularly popular evangelicalism—in North America. Megachurch hype is leading a majority of Americans to overdefine the success of megachurches and underdefine the true picture of a rapidly diminishing Christianity. In 1995 Marva Dawn warned us of being deceived by these apparent pictures of success. David Barrett reported statistics for Oxford University Press that in a twelve-month period, 2,765,100 worship attenders in Europe and North America cease to be practicing Christians—an average loss of 7,600 every day. This means that every week more than 53,000 people leave churches and never come back. The percentage of active Christians in the West has fallen from 29.0 percent in 1900 to 23.3 percent of today's population . . . . We must ask why, "despite glowing reports of surging church attendance, more and more Christians in North America are feeling *disillusioned* with the church."[13]

‡Marva Dawn warned us further that the assumption by such pollsters as George Barna seems to indicate that bigger churches often have a worship form that is full of joy. The corollary is that contemporary forms furnish such joy. But do bigger churches necessarily create happier pastors? "Barna's work is immensely appealing; it is full of love for unbelievers and offers great suggestions for reaching out to the world. However, we must read his work with discernment because of his lack of emphasis on the truth side of the dialectic . . . . Barna seems to have fallen into the present culture's idolatry of happiness."[14]

§Pastors are ever more the victims of downwardly spiraling self-esteem. Sam's need to think well of himself is a common need among America's church leaders. Some years ago Robert Schuller wrote a book called *Self-Esteem: a New Reformation.* It was his contention at the time that evangelicals rated lowest of all cultural groups in thinking well of themselves. If that was true of church members as a whole, it must be even truer of pastors. Churches are places of conflict, and much of the time in any such conflict, the pastors come up the losers. Guy Greenfield put it this way: "Church conflict is a normal part of most churches. Yet there has been an alarming increase in the number of churches experiencing mean-spirited individuals who antagonize and seek the eventual termination of unsuspecting pastors. A national survey in *Leadership* magazine reported that 23% of ministers had been fired at least once and 43% stated that they had been forced to resign because of a 'faction.' Of the churches who fired a pastor, a staggering 41% did so at least twice.

The care group for Zone 3 could visit her.* Sam played on. This was what God intended. The care committee was there to care, while Sam improved his swing. Will Willington was a genius.

He set the ball on the tee. This ball had a little red dot on it, so he could always find it. It was his long ball. He had named it the Emma Johnson Special. He loved putting it on the tee and then driving it far away into the sky, out among the planets, so he could succeed, succeed, succeed. Had not Will said, "Succeed, succeed, succeed, cry a grand 'Whalloop!' and then succeed some more"?[†] He studied the little ball as it set on the tee. He thought of Emma Johnson, with her long flouncy curls and her little wire glasses—trifocals they were—a trinitarian metaphor divided into three parts in one pair of glasses. "Vengeance is mine sayeth me and the Lord. Whammo Emma!" said Sam as he swung the number 9 iron. Off flew Emma into the ether above the country club. Life was as it should be. The bluebird of happiness was whistling two and three choruses in the underbrush.[‡]

As soon as the morning round was over, Sam had a long, lingering Pepsi at the clubhouse. He was going to be taking a lot of long, lingering Pepsis now that the new zonal care groups were in charge of all things desperate. No more would the sick and suffering keep him from his destiny. He was megabound.

Just before the meeting of the new pastoral care committee, Sam was feeling great. He was on the way to Mega. All his life, he had been Mini, but now Mega was looming on the horizon.[§] The kingdom of God was green as Canaan. Life was milk and honey. Sinai was past. He had moved from the deserts of Zin into the Nazarene Neo. The spies were back with telephone surveys of greater Canaan. Rumpton Rill Community Church was on the way just as surely as the sick were out of the way. Sam's march into the land of milk and honey had begun.

13

When a minister is forced from a pastorate because of a conflict, the minister's family, the church body, and the witness of the church all suffer."

Author Guy Greenfield, who is also a "wounded minister," calls those laypersons who hurt or abuse ministers "clergy killers." Greenfield also offers encouragement to other wounded ministers as well as remedies for healing people and congregations.[15]

Sam's fault, however, may be in thinking that bigger churches make happier pastors. Such may or may not be the case. Still, in speaking to scores of pastors' conferences across the years, I find the myth still persisting that I would be happier if only my church were bigger.

*It is typical of us that we often want to imagine some technique as the goose that laid the golden egg. Eugene Peterson would correct Sam in counting too much on the latest published technique to deliver him. Leadership is far more than copying somebody else's good ideas, and techniques are not sacred. Nor are they efficacious from one situation to another to deliver us. "There is a great deal of advice given today," writes Peterson, "about cultivating leadership. There is a popular journal with that title, *Leadership*. Counsel in how to be leaders is unending, but it all has to be tested against our scriptures. There are a lot of good ideas out there, but when they take over the core of what we're doing, we end up in the Gulag, enduring an unrecognized persecution. Against all leadership counsel we have to set Jesus, and not so much to figure out how to be leaders from what he said and did but enter into the world that he lived in, the relationships that he cultivated, and assimilate his style. This leadership is not techniques and strategies called from a superficial reading of the Gospels that knows little of Jesus himself, but a Jesus-leadership spirit, mind, sensitivity. It is a leadership that is conspicuously lacking in the exercise of power and the attraction of followers."[16]

†It is difficult in a materialist world for pastors to avoid the typical desire to get better paid. Often they are poorly compensated for the work they do. Sometimes this low pay can whet the preacher's attitude for better pay. The golden calf always stands across from the risen Christ and beckons to the needy and devoted leaders of the church. It is not just the wealthy pastor who makes idolatry of need and the material things that beg to fill it. Chuck Pierce wrote, "Money and wealth have inherent power; if you do not bring that power under the subjection of the Holy Spirit, it will overwhelm and ensnare you."[17]

No more manna. Manna was the food of the minipastor. Those content to live in Canaan. Now Sam was seated in the palace making decisions. Instead of letting other people run his life, he was running theirs. This was just as God intended it to be. There were plenty of evidences he was in God's will. He had lost five pounds and had just bought himself two new Tommy Bahama shirts, the new clerical robes of suburban churchdom.

Sam found himself whistling "The Impossible Dream" as he drove toward the church for his first zonal compassion meeting.* He stopped at Wal-Mart and bought saddle wax to shine up his golf bag after he got home from the committee meeting at the church.

It was a glorious day. Sam actually began to sing: "To dream the impossible dream, To drown in a sweet bowl of cream, To golf while the laity suffers ... hmmm, humm." Sam kept on humming, unable to think of the original lyrics until he got to the chorus. "This is my quest, to stick out my chest, and golf at my best, while all of the suffering lie somewhere out west." It was not a great rendition, but Sam sang it loudly.

He pulled up at a stop sign, still singing. While he waited for the light he noticed the man next to him was driving a Kia. He had seen Sam's exhibitionist singing and looked at him in a bemused fashion. This unsettled Sam a bit. Until he saw the man smirking over his animated singing. The man's snobbish deportment ticked Sam off. When the light changed, he stomped the accelerator and whizzed across the intersection well ahead of the Kia. *Kia,* thought Sam. *The next time I leave you in the dust, Buster, I'll be driving a Lexus.*†

Sam's behavior wasn't very pastoral. But the situation was worse than that. He suddenly realized that the driver of the Kia was Earl Payton. Good grief! How could he have been so stupid?

*Sam's most serious mistake may be in believing that all things concerning pastoral care can be delegated. Of course they cannot. No true minister of God can delegate the alleviation of suffering to a committee and then declare, "There now! That's done with!" Erwin McManus writes, "The life of the church is the heart of God. The heart of God is to serve a broken world . . . . The serving we are called to do requires direct contact. You cannot wash the feet of the dirty world if you refuse to touch it."[18]

†Emma has a point. For Pastor Sam not to see that is indeed disgraceful. We have had plenty of banter about church growth evangelism versus pastoral care. But no matter how large a church grows, the church that only gets big but will not care for the sick and broken, is no church of Christ. As important as world evangelization was to Jesus, the Gospels are filled with his compassion for the sick and dying. No legitimate pastor can delegate this concern. He may delegate the care of a specific person in need, but the moment he tries to delegate the concern, the church he pastors will be gone.

Erwin McManus, in his very balanced cry for church growth and compassions says, "It is in serving that the church finds her strength. When she ceases to serve the world around her, she begins to atrophy. In pathology, atrophy is the wasting or decreasing in size of any part of a body. When the church refuses to serve the world, she begins to waste away. She finds herself deteriorating, withering, and losing her strength. Like a muscle that has been locked away in a cast, the church shows the signs of atrophy that become evident when the cast is removed. It is difficult to ignore the reality that the church has lost significant muscle tissue. All around us we find evidence that the church of Jesus Christ in our contemporary society is not what she once was."[19]

Earl was on the way to church too. And worse than that, he was on one of the zonal care committees.

Sam beat him to the church parking lot and was comfortably inside the church when it suddenly occurred to him what his real problem was: Emma Johnson was the chairperson of the new zonal care committee.* Sam thought of her. He tried to say the word *mega,* but the word stuck in his throat. Emma was the megaboondoggle in his pathway to success.

Sam joined the committee and sat at the corner of the table, on the same side of the table as Earl Payton. So he wouldn't have to look at him. The one time he did catch sight of him, Earl was grinning—but too broadly! Sam felt relieved. At least Earl wasn't taking it seriously, or was he?

Emma Johnson called the meeting to order.

"Pastor, our new zonal care committee has three problems."

"Only three. That's wonderful, Emma," said Sam.

"Wonderful, yes, but these problems are serious."

Sam didn't know what the problems were, or how serious they could be.

"First," said Emma, "Carl Wilson has been in the hospital for seven days and nobody has been to visit. I'd call that disgraceful."†

"Why has nobody been to see him?" asked Sam.

"It's because he lives on 32nd Street. And, Pastor, as you know, that's the dividing line between Zones 3 and 4. Now just whose responsibility is it when a person needs pastoral care and lives on the dividing line between two zones? Pastor Willington doesn't give us an answer to this in the chapter called "Zonify or Die." What am I supposed to do, Pastor? I didn't feel like I could ask Charlie's care group because they have already had one appendicitis and Esther's latest ectomy. You know she had her . . . well, I don't think we should say out loud what Esther Thompson had taken out, even if

*Sam's mistake may be in thinking one can be so committee-driven and mechanical about pastoral care. To care for others in need is more mystical and inward. We never care in any outer way until we have subjected the needs of others to the inner Christ. Again Eugene Peterson has influenced my view of pastoral care: "The understanding and conviction that bring us together in this book are that pastoral work originates in and is shaped by the revelation of God in Jesus Christ. It takes place in the world's culture, but it is not caused by it. It is intimately involved in the world, but it is not defined by it. The gospel is free, not only in the sense that we don't have to pay for it, but also in the more fundamental sense that it is an expression of God's freedom—it is not caused by our needs but by God's grace."[20]

†The stigma that Christians use to mark gays not only marks them as homophobic but eliminates all possibility of ministering to them. Perhaps what needs to occur is the church being overtly open in its concern for all social stigmas and seeking to redeem the world in every need. I recommend William Webb's book, *Slaves, Women and Homosexuals,* a 2001 InterVarsity Press release, for further thoughtful study in the matter.

it hadn't been of much use to her recently. But, Pastor, can't you see that the committee really has all they can handle. I wonder if you would mind calling on all the sick who live on zone lines?"

Emma looked at Sam. Sam looked down. He knew what was about to happen. Emma was very forceful when she made decisions.

"Yes," she said. "Now I proclaim new committee rule number 1: If anyone who lives on a zone line gets sick, the pastor will be responsible for their care. Agreed?"

The committee quickly agreed.*

Sam groaned. "What's the other problem?" he asked.

"Well, Bobby Jones cracked three ribs at football practice, and Deacon Simpson on Care Group 2 won't go see him."

"Why not? Deacon Simpson, why will you not go?" asked Sam, looking directly at him.

"It's them earrings!" blurted out Deacon Simpson. "Bobby Jones must be sexually unsure of himself or he wouldn't be wearing earrings. I think that's why the good Lord gave him a case of cracked ribs. He's just not tough enough for the football team."†

"Bobby Jones? That's preposterous! A lot of guys wear earrings," protested Sam. "Why shouldn't we show him the same love God shows us?"

"Because earring guys are always flaky and very libertine! I could get an STD," said the deacon, as if he hadn't heard Sam.

Sam almost laughed. He wondered if the old deacon could even think wild enough to get an STD. Even inoculations would be unnecessary. While thus he mused, Emma rapped the gravel once again.

"I proclaim committee rule number 2: Any sick man who wears earrings will henceforward become the pastor's responsibility. Now for our third problem. Grace MacDonald, tell the pastor your problem."

*The ministry of pastoral care is a ministry that not so much welcomes tears as it welcomes a person's right to cry. And the ministry of the church ought to realize that tears are the condition of the world. And it may not be to the church's credit that she has not learned to weep with those who weep. Jonah in the Old Testament sinned the sin of so many modern churchmen. He lost the ability to weep over what God wept over. Thomas Carlyle said:

> The word came
> and he went
> in the other
> direction.
> God said: Cry
> tears of compassion
> tears of repentance; cry against
> the reek
> of unrighteousness; cry for
> the right turn
> the contrite spirit.
> and Jonah rose
> and fled
> in tearless silence.[21]

†It seems that almost any attempts at anything noble, including love and pastoral care, are always challenged immediately by our propensity toward hating others who are in the same business with us. I was always amazed as a pastor how quickly the flock lost their ability to focus on the work of God because of their need to get the credit for some "Christian venture" or to express their vengeance toward somebody who professed to love Christ just as they did and get the credit for it all. I do believe that many a pastor has looked around at congregational pettiness and asked himself, "What am I doing among the wolves teaching the ways of sheep?" James A. Harnish wrote:

> Where do you find the power to hang in there in this world?
> Where do you find the power to keep going
> when the going really gets tough?
> Where do you find the power to continue
> to believe in love in a world that's filled with hate?
> Where do we find the power to continue to work for peace
> in a world addicted to violence?
> Where do we find the power to continue to believe in good
> in a world that is filled with so much suffering and pain?
> Where do we find the power to continue
> to believe that ultimately God's kingdom will come
> and God's will, as revealed in Jesus, will be done in all of the creation?
> Where do you find the power to be a disciple of Jesus in this world?[22]

"Well, Pastor," Grace offered timidly, "when I went to Deaconess Hospital to see Tom Caruthers, he was in a terrible state. His depression causes him to cry a lot. It just made me too sad. I am not good with men who cry. I just didn't know what to do.* So I just left the devotional guide with him and said, 'Now, now, dearie, don't cry.'"

"Then what happened?" asked Sam.

"He said, 'Don't call me *dearie,* please.' In my opinion he was just too bossy for a sick man. Then I started crying, and there we were, both of us crying, when the doctor came in and asked if I needed someone in therapy. Then I really cried and ran out of the room. I cried the rest of the afternoon. I won't go back. I won't! Emma, could we move him to Zone 2 and let Zelpha Anderson go see him?"

"Oh no, you don't!" cried Zelpha from Zone 2. "The only thing I know to do is take people casseroles, and I've found that when people cry all the time they don't eat very well. No, no, you don't, Grace MacDonald! You just keep your own depressives in your own zone." Zelpha thought for a moment and then added, "Did you try baking him a casserole?"

"Yes, I took him one last week."

"Dearie, I hate to tell you this. That could have been the reason for Tom's depression. I've eaten your casseroles and—"

"Now, now. Everybody cool down.† We can solve this problem," said Emma. "Grace, I can understand why you don't feel comfortable calling on crying men. I wouldn't either. But the answer is not moving people around from zone to zone. There's a more sensible way to solve this. Sam, I'm going to rule that there are three special cases where you will have to give the zonal care committees a little special help. These are my three committee rules I proclaim: All sick people who live on zone lines, boys with earrings, and depressive men will in every case revert to the responsibility of the pastor."

I have never believed that the ministerial dropout or burnout rate is related to the work of pastoral care, but only to the infighting among the saints who ought to be devoted to pastoral care.

*The problem with Sam's assumption here is rooted in the notion that a pastor's main responsibility is the sermon. The importance of the sermon cannot be dismissed, but it still is second to the pastor's commitment to live in the world and represent at every moment of the week the will of the Savior. The "ego rewards" of preaching may have deluded us into believing that it is the only important work of the pastor. This would be no more true of the pastor than it was of Jesus. We do not remember Jesus primarily because he gave himself to the technicalities of sermon writing. No, we remember Jesus because he was the incarnation of God. All that he was in any moment—in a preaching mode or out of one—was the Son of God, playing the servant of every circumstance. The pastor's life is never just the show-off work of preaching.

Erwin McManus, who has become for me a sensible model of all that's most compassionate and informed, puts all the sentiments of pastoral care into one category—the heart of God: "The life of the church is the heart of God. The heart of God is to serve a broken world. When Jesus wrapped a towel around his waist, he reminded us that only he could wash away our sin. The church cannot live when the heart of God is not beating within her. God's heartbeat is to seek and save that which is lost. The church exists to serve as the body of Christ, and it is through this commitment to serve that we are forced to engage our culture."[23]

And just how do we engage our culture? Not primarily through sermons, I think. Rather, through the demonstration of compassion—in things like mastering the art of pastoral care.

†There is a severe legalism in the making of assignments to be compassionate. As long as caring can be delegated by cards and lay assignments, it probably has no real existence. Lately, the brilliant mystic Raniero Cantalamessa has influenced me. He reminds me that man-made structures can only result in human contrivances that fall short of all we are when our ministry to others is driven by the Holy Spirit. Cantalamessa says, "The natural religiosity of man, that which he creates following his own sentiment, aims at a sort of high pyramid—made in some cases of intellectual and speculative powers . . . . But the Bible has revealed to us something quite different. By becoming flesh God has overturned the pyramid, has descended, has put himself at the bottom and supports all of us with his grace."[24]

"Wait a minute," cried Sam. "We started this zonal care program so I could become more of a preaching pastor and spend a lot more time in my study."*

"Yes," agreed Emma, "but there must always be these three special areas where you help out. Just these three, Pastor. Surely you can help a little with the sick."

"So if I do these three kinds of cases, will the zonal care committees do the rest?"

"Yes."

"Always?"

"Ever and ever, world without end," agreed Emma.

"But what about William Pence," asked Grace MacDonald. "He's not in my zone, but if he were, I wouldn't feel comfortable visiting him. He's got these little skin sores on his face. It's horrible. He's the ugliest man you can see for free. I just can't look at him. 'Course, lucky for me, he's not in my care zone, but what if he were?"

Emma paused and thought it over. "I now proclaim my fourth rule: All Zone 3 people with skin sores will also be the responsibility of the pastor."

Sam groaned again. "That's all then. These are the four special cases!"†

"That's all." Emma was firm this time.

"But what about Old Kate in Golden Home?" said Ben Allred, who had sat fairly quiet through most of the meeting. "Old Kate's in my zone. I took her some chocolate-covered peanuts 'cause she told me she likes 'em. She doesn't like 'em at all. She likes to suck the chocolate off of 'em. She only has three teeth; can you imagine how disgusting that is?"

Sam could imagine it. Emma couldn't, but she could see that they had already made enough work for Sam. She immediately took Sam's side on this one. "I'm sorry, but I must make one more

*Mother Teresa of Calcutta taught us that we were only mature in faith when we could see the sufferings as the Lord himself. Sam has obviously not matured to the point where he sees that pastoral care of the needy is a ministry unto Christ himself. So he resents his assignment and his ministry. Francis of Assisi knew that maturity that relished ministry. He said, "When I was in the bondage of sin, it was bitter and loathsome to me to look upon those infected with leprosy, but the blessed Lord brought me among them: and when I departed from them, what seemed bitter and loathsome was turned and changed to me into great sweetness and comfort, both of body and soul." How wonderful God must regard pastors who turn toward pastoral care, for they have learned to consider their ministry to the broken as service given directly to Christ![25]

†The world is ever open to true God lovers. Why? Because there is an unwritten law that suspects that anyone really in love with God is bent on loving his world. "A community with the servant heart of God knows no limit to sacrifice, and when its people are doing what God created them to do, there is no limit to impact."[26]

ruling: I proclaim that old peanut suckers are the responsibility of the care zone in which they suck, and they may neither be moved to another zone nor be laid upon the pastor."

Sam felt a little better but not for long.

"OK then! I am quitting this committee. See how you like that, Emma Johnson."

Ben Allred stomped out of the committee room.

There was silence for awhile, until Emma regained her composure. "I must now make one final ruling," said Emma. "I now proclaim that in the case of a care group member who leaves the committee for any reason, the responsibilities of that position will be incumbent upon the pastor until such time as the position can be refilled. Sam—"

"I'll take Kate her peanuts." Sam was clearly miffed.[*]

"Is there anything else?" asked Emma.

"Yes," said Earl Payton. "Pastor, why did you send Baxter to make calls in Zone 2?"

"Baxter?" asked Sam.

"I didn't meet him personally, but Tom Caruthers said he was a very prissy fellow with an English accent. Is he a friend of yours, Sam?" asked Earl, in a tone that proved he was still miffed at Sam for the drag race at the stop sign an hour earlier.

"No, Earl, I didn't send any English fellow, and I haven't the slightest idea what you're talking about."

"Well, Pastor, Caruthers said he opened up his King James Bible and read him a verse or two and then prayed, like he was King James himself. He even sounded like the original King James. Caruthers said he was a wonderfully nice man. He was warm and personable, and really a good church visitor. He said that the man really seemed to know and love God and that he was wonderfully refreshed by his manner."[†]

*Every act of pastoral care must remind the suffering that suffering, however it may seem, is not for long. Charles P. Schmitt offers a prayer that ought to be the common currency of all who minister to hurt with hope: "Father, You know the losses I have sustained. Work with me that I may gladly consider everything a loss compared to the surpassing greatness of knowing Christ Jesus my Lord. I open wide my heart so that Jesus may be revealed in me; I want to know Him and share in His sufferings so that His powerful resurrection life might flow out of me! For His sake. Amen."[27]

†The "success syndrome" builds many rationales. Is it possible that many success-driven pastors rationalize their lack of pastoral care by agreeing that it is better to preach to many than pastorally serve a few? "The world invites us to climb ladders," writes Leonard Sweet. "The gospel invites us to lift crosses."[28] Leonard Sweet refers to this "need to be seen" kind of ministry as "playing large." He says, "playing large" has replaced "working hard" as the ultimate compliment.[29] I have stood back and tried to see the big picture in the kingdom of God. It is easy for me to understand that some people—dare I suggest cable TV evangelists—get through with a little truth to a lot of people. Others—shall I cite a hero of mine, Charles Swindoll—get through to less people with a whole lot of truth. But it seems to me in the era of megachurch we have opted to tell smaller truths to ever-bigger crowds. Eugene Peterson once said, "The greater the truth the smaller the crowd." I believe he is right. Yet between the question of whether we shall preach to a few or to a great many lies the issue of our ego and image. And we had rather see ourselves in large ways than actually live them out.

"You know, Earl, I wouldn't put a lot of stock in what Tom Caruthers says. He went to the hospital because he was having psychological problems."

"Yes, but he gave me this . . ." Earl extended a yellowed piece of paper to Sam.

Sam took it.

"Read it. . . . Read it to all of us."

Sam at first determined not to do it but then thought better of it and began to read:

> Is sickness too much with thee?
> Look to him whose healing is forever.
> Weeping only beckons night
> So touch the Christ and wait for light.*

"Well, it would seem whoever Baxter is, he's a poet," Sam said.

Sam left the meeting and got in his car to drive home. It was after dinner on Monday night when he decided to do a little more reading from *You Too Can Be a Megaman of God.* He read the final chapter over again: "Free from the Needs of the Few to Serve the Many."† In many ways it seemed to Sam he would never be free from the needs of the few. Sam wondered how Will Willington had ever broken free.

Sam had never been to a Willington Megaman Conference, so he was glad that on the following week he was going to be at a special downlinked simulcast where he would at least get to see Willington on video. Willington had said that only the feeblest of preachers tried to *carpé* the *diem.* The key to vital ministry was to try to *carpé mañana.* If they could *carpé mañana* they could *carpé* a lot of things. Indeed. So Sam was determined that at this simulcast he would try to *carpé mañana* as best he could.

*The "heavy burden of getting ahead" that Richard Foster talks about often takes an especially heavy burden on the striving for success to which many a megachurch wannabe has dedicated himself. Unfortunately many congregations want to be this frenzied model. "Congregations want pastors who will lead them in the world of religious competition," writes Eugene Peterson.[30] Church growth is noble only when it results from a God-given vision of transformation. It is never noble when it arises from a spirit of pastoral competition.

†One of our Baptist forebears was credited with saying Baptists are many but not much. Leonard Sweet reminds us that big can be either bad or good. But small is best. The average business of the future will be three people.[31] We cannot say that a megachurch is godly just because it's bigger. By such logic Woodstock would be more godly than Pentecost. We do know that, large or small, the only successful church is possessed of a dream of transformation: "The church according to Paul was to be a people destined to be a revolutionary movement that ultimately invades all societal institutions, and transforms them into what God wanted them to be (Eph. 1:22)."[32]

Early the next morning Sam went to the Bread Box, a local restaurant to have breakfast with two fellow ministers. He was there well ahead of them and managed to read the sports section of the newspaper always graciously supplied by the restaurant for its customers. But he hadn't gotten very far into it when Father Ambrose arrived. Sam really liked the Episcopal priest and admired him for many reasons. Still, Sam saw him as even worse off than he was. One of the most troubling things about the priest was that he really wasn't trying to make his church grow.* And it probably wasn't going to happen.

He still insisted on visiting the sick of his parish. He would not zonify. Therefore all he could do was die. Actually he didn't even seem to care about it. He went around saying Latin-like things that made him look like an atheist to others. There were other problems that kept his church from growing. How could he hope to have a good reputation if he wasn't trying to *carpé* things? Sam knew his church wasn't growing either, but at least he was doing his part in trying to please God by feeling neurotic about it. They had barely had time to greet each other when Biff Wheeler came in.

Oh, his entrance both inflated and deflated Sam. There he was: Ralph Lauren slacks, one-hundred-dollar Hush Puppies, a Tommy Bahama shirt, three pounds of mousse on his ruthless hair, and he smelled of Chrome Azarro. No wonder his church was growing. He was the perfect blend of John the Baptist and Versace.

"Hey, Sam! Hey, Ambrose! How many did you have in church yesterday?" Biff asked.

"All that God wanted me to have, and not a single communicant, besides," answered Father Ambrose, who didn't like to give Biff the advantage of one-upping him.†

It bugged Biff that Ambrose preferred calling his members communicants instead of adherents, which was the megachurch way.

*Os Guinness verbally whips evangelicals in *Fit Bodies, Fat Minds* for having "buns of steel and minds of silly putty." We are the outside people; like movie sets, we're all painted veneer and all façade. Nothing exists behind our appearances. What you see is all there is. In a world where appearance is everything, Evangelicals have agreed to be shallow to win the shallow. What they will never agree to is looking bad in a world where looks are everything. Guinness says, "An hour or two a day, five times a week, like medieval monks visiting the stations of the cross, our Nautilus men move from machine to machine as they work on their abdomen, hips, buttocks, quadriceps, calves, backs, shoulders, chests, triceps and biceps . . . . Style, style, style—style is a leading currency in modern society, the river of life for American consumerism, the main artery of American identity and belonging." It is small wonder that Harvey Cox spoke of the captivity of the American church. Truly we have proven ourselves captive to toothpaste commercials and health spas. If we have any urgent authenticity of our own, we have seldom revealed it. Our churches, like our corporations, want to be larger and pretty much for the same reasons. How we need an authentic vision. To get large because it is a goal is indeed to live chained to the worst sort of smallness. Our captivity to style is only the furthest reach of our pseudo *rasion d'etre.*[33]

†"Religion," says Richard Rohr, "has not tended to create seekers or searchers, has not tended to create honest, humble people who trust that God is always beyond them. We aren't focused on the great mystery. Religion has, rather, tended to create people who think they have God in their pockets, people with quick, easy, glib answers. That's why so much of the West is understandably abandoning religion." We shall not in the end be able to continue the great church growth trend. The YMCA tried this approach 150 years ago. While they succeeded as a community entity, they failed as a Christian movement. Business and involvement can never compensate for the place of the mystery of godliness in the human spirit.[34]

"How about you, Sam?"

"Oh, we had 392, if you count the five who came in late and slept through the sermon. The Billingsleys always play pinochle with the Comptons on Saturday night clear through to the wee hours of Sunday morning. Then they all get to church late and sleep through the sermon."

"Three-ninety-two! Want to know how many we had?"

Ambrose didn't.

Sam didn't either.

"3,487! How are you guys, anyway?"

"Any chance you could ask how we are before you ask how many we had in church?" asked Ambrose. "There's a part of me that wants to tell you how I'm doing before I tell you how big the crowd was. *Miserere Domine!* Anyway, I happen to be doing fine."

"Me too," said Sam. "And Biff, I'm looking forward to the Will Willington simulcast next week. I have just finished reading, *You Too Can Be a Megaman of God.*"

"PTL, Sam. That's awesome. Isn't that just the coolest book since the 'Right Behind' novels." Biff flashed that million-dollar smile. It was obvious that he had just had his teeth whitened.* The white glare from his mouth was all but blinding as he said, "We signed up 143 decision cards at the end of the service. Boy, do we have a rockin' flock! But I prefer the word *herd* more than the word *flock.* You know Willington. He says that shepherds and flocks are not how we think anymore. I'm not a shepherd. I'm a rancher."

"Yippee-kay-aye-ay!" quipped Father Ambrose.

"Laugh if you will, but if the flow of new members doesn't slow down before long we'll have to form another new softball league.† Our fourth new league since January! Oh, the pressures of a growing church! You wanna know how much moola they dumped in the coffers?"

*There is a smugness that many fast-growing independent churches often hold toward old-line denominational churches, but this smugness is unjustified. Willimon and Campolo believe that many megachurch converts turn at last to the traditional church "because they come to the place where sectarian Christianity no longer speaks to them. Liturgical Christianity can be very real to those who appreciate being connected to creedal traditions that are solid and secure. They enjoy the historic hymns that connect them with the saints of the past and give them assurances of the future."[35] I recently attended an Episcopal church and was struck by the huge amount of Scripture used in the service. Nearly a hundred verses of Scripture were used in that single service. I couldn't help but feel a strong sense of biblical authority that my own denomination sometimes boasts about but rarely demonstrates to that degree. It is this dimension that ultimately leads many megachurch members to stop cherishing size and begin craving content. It is in this spirit that Tom Howard names his book, *Evangelical Is Not Enough.* Greatness of size may, in the end, prove the smallest of virtues.

Sam didn't.

Ambrose didn't.

"Well, I can tell I'm overwhelming you dudes, so I won't lay it on you. Let's just say it was all five digits . . . before the decimal point! You could hear the angels sing their bank draft alleluias!"

"So that's where the angels were—passing your plates. They didn't even hum the doxology at our church," said Ambrose.

"Father Ambrose, you ought to swallow your Episcopal pride and come to our Willington simulcast next week. We'd have you out of that black collar and into Tommy Bahama before you know it. Is there any rule in your church that says you gotta be a Zorro look-alike all the time? You'd stick out like a sore thumb at Hooters. Besides, you can't serve the uppertaker dressed like an undertaker."

Ambrose ignored the cliché.

"Hey, Biff, Father Ambrose is all right just as he is."

"Well, maybe, but not a single one of the new megachurches is Episcopal. Now how do you figure it?"*

"Well, Biff, I think we Episcopalians treasure the inner life. We treasure Christian heritage. We have a history and a millennium-long tradition of liturgy and prayer. You want to know what I most resent about these community megachurches?"

Biff didn't.

"These churches all seem to feel that the centuries between the time of Christ, the founder, and the time they started were just empty years of nothing. Now take your hero—yours and Sam's—Will Willington."

Sam shifted nervously. Biff froze.

Ambrose marched on. "It's like there wasn't any history. Nothing was going on since the close of the New Testament era. It's like God and the angels and the human race all just lapsed into a coma somewhere back in the first century and didn't snap

*Many modern evangelicals have sought for the depth that is offered them in the more liturgical church. This was certainly the experience of Thomas Howard. "Accustomed to the informal worship of evangelicalism, Thomas Howard was intrigued by the ritual and ceremony of his first liturgical church encounter as a teen-ager. It was an experience he never forgot. Today, as an adult, Howard has learned to appreciate the worship practices of the liturgical church. In fact, after long and painful soul searching, he admits that these practices provide much needed help in his communion with God: 'Centuries of Christian wisdom and practice . . . direct and give shape to my weak and helter-skelter resources of self-discipline and concentration.'"[36]

†The answer to whether or not Christianity should contemporize or traditionalize is probably neither. Both of these pastors state the obvious end of the churches who stand at the poles of the question. It was Alexander Pope who cautioned us against these extremes when he wrote,
"Be not the first by which the new is tried,
Nor yet the last to lay the old aside."

Ed Young Jr. expresses for all who take the contemporary road the severest of warnings: "Visuals can be illuminating. Videos can move and inspire. Lights and props and drama can keep people interested. But too much of a good thing can quickly distract from the very reason that people need to be there, which is to apply the word of God to their lives."[37]

out of it until Will Willington arose in New Jersey, like a con-
quistador, to plant the flag of the faith in the middle of a thousand softball leagues."*

"Now wait just a cotton-pickin' minute!" shouted Biff. "We're
vaguely aware of Billy Graham. And what was the name of that
woman back in the twenties that started the Angelus Temple?
We've heard of D. L. Moody. We know our Christian history."

"Ever heard of Augustine?" answered Sam.

"You mean that city in Florida where the Mets do their winter
training?"

"Well, the city was named after him, but the man himself
lived a long time ago. And do your people know about him? Do
Will Willington's people?

"Well, do your people know about Mel Kitt and the Gospel
Kats."

"No."

"Well, there you go. We're equal. You see, Ambrose, if every
church was like yours, the Christian faith wouldn't be here in fifty
years."

"And if every church was like yours, it wouldn't be historically
Christian in fifty years. No one would be left who can even define
the word *Christian*.† The faith would die of a secular syncretism."

"Syncre what!"

"Syncretism. It's what happens when Jesus marries the culture, and they return from their honeymoon to la-la land to settle
down and raise unholy children."

Biff could not track the conversation. Church history was difficult. That was why Biff dropped out of college to go into the
ministry.

"Biff, do you know what the YMCA was saying in 1850?"

It was pretty clear Biff didn't know YMCA existed in 1850.

*This point was made in an earlier footnote, and, at the risk of being redundant, I would remind the reader that Christianity has only a few possible positions to take in reference to culture, enumerated long ago by Richard Neibuhr. The church may stand against culture which cuts down its opportunity to redeem it. Or it may embrace culture and risk being changed by it, and these changes may indeed complicate if not decimate the truth of the gospel. The Easter bunny remains a strong reminder that the most pagan of cultural concepts can become a part of the faith or at least a part of the way that we situate faith in culture. Let us not forget that Hegel's reminder of all encounters is thesis, antithesis, and synthesis. Mircea Eliade reminds us in *Sacred and the Profane* that the first telltale sign that a faith's force is over in a culture is when there is no longer a distinct difference between the sound and appearance of the sacred—our very ability to distinguish—and the sound and appearance of the profane. See Richard Niebuhr's *Christ and Culture* and Mircea Eliade's *Sacred and the Profane.*

†This is a dimension of pastoral care that actually happened to me when one of my members from our smaller church in Omaha joined a megachurch in a distant city. I was so surprised when he called me and asked me to perform his wedding. His own pastor was far too busy, he said. We also had the wedding in a smaller denominational church because the chapel of the megachurch was schedule-locked to their finest, most faithful members.

"Well, back then the YMCA was a very hot, Christian evangelistic organization. In 1850 it was trying to get the whole world saved and was preaching, 'Come with us and play basketball and we'll talk about Jesus.' But by 1950 it was just saying 'come and play basketball with us.' I believe the megachurch hasn't got enough theology to last into the next century. It has gone around asking people what kind of church they want, and then they build it. Funny, they never check in with God to see what kind of church he wants and build that kind of church. Further, it is not a church schooled in suffering. Where are its martyrs, its people who have paid to belong to the church? They're all young. If the 'Right Behind' novels are right, they are all expecting Jesus to show up and whisk them out of the culture just before Armageddon. They not only have never been schooled in suffering; they follow a Savior who wants to pamper them with cross-less religion, right up to the trumpet blast. But most of all, you know what I resent . . ."*

Biff had now been backed into the corner. It seemed Ambrose's hot breath was melting Biff's mousse and some of his longer hair had collapsed over his right eye. "No . . . no, I don't," said Biff, somewhat more timidly. It was the first time Sam had never seen a megachurch pastor groveling before an advancing Episcopalian.

"I don't like their lack of a wholistic view of life. What happens when megachurch members get sick or die? They all do sooner or later, you know. Everybody needs a pastor when they are sick, and I'm not so sure the 'staff'—a megapastor euphemism for 'Let George do it'—can supply the need of so many. The world is full of hurt; it needs a pastor. Further, I know of three people in this town who are members of your church who couldn't get married in your church—and they wanted to—because your chapel was booked too far ahead. Now is that right? You can't marry all your members because you have too many members?"†

*In the final analysis, the small pastor's flagging self-esteem may be a major motivator toward the building of a megachurch. Of course, the sensitive and wonderful ministers of the megachurch would decry this. But I suspect a great killer of local pastors is the drudgery of trying to do God's work without a word of appreciation. The pastors of today are dying for want of appreciation. In effect their pastoral care adds up to nothing.

†All of our pastoral care is for Jesus. It is indeed his blood which commissions us. We tend to forget that, says Max Lucado: "Our hearts are good; it is just that our memories are bad. We forget how significant one touch can be. We fear saying the wrong thing or using the wrong word tone or acting the wrong way . . . . Keep in mind the perspective of the lepers of the world. They aren't picky. They aren't finicky. They're just lonely. They are yearning for a godly touch."[38]

Biff was quiet.

Sam was quiet.

"You wanted to know how many I had in church, last Sunday, Biff. I'll tell you how many. All I can take care of."

Things were quiet for awhile.

Sam finally cleared his throat and began the conversation again. "Father Ambrose, sometimes I feel like you, but I get no respect. I think if I were more like Biff, maybe people would look up to me."*

Biff said nothing.

Ambrose said, "Sam, 'Me' is a little reason for doing anything. I don't know if I get a lot of respect either. Still, if I wanted respect I'd go into politics." Ambrose stopped again, and Sam could nearly watch his mind as it turned a brighter corner. He was about to change the subject.

"Sam, I met your friend Baxter at the hospital this week," Ambrose continued. "He said he was helping you by calling on your members. He knew you were busy. A most delightful man. Very English. How did you ever make his acquaintance?" But before Sam could answer, Ambrose went on. Drawing a piece of paper from his pocket, he handed it to Sam and said, "He gave me this."

Sam took the paper and read.

> Touch a hurting child and thou walkest Galilee.
> Then shalt thou serve the hand-nailed king
> Whose blood commissions thee.†

"Does Baxter make your hospital rounds often for you?"

Sam was quiet.

Not Biff. "Hey, Sam, maybe he could make your hospital calls while you're at the Willington simulcast next week."

"Maybe," said Sam.

*Some of the various forms of worship or church programs deserve a great deal of inspection before we give them our approval. Max Lucado tells of William Rathje, a Harvard-educated "garbologist" who has made a life of looking at garbage and its cultural implications. From the junk of a culture, we can tell just how junky a culture is. From what we throw away (or ought to) we can tell the nature of our way of life.[39] Lucado doesn't go into worship or pastoral care at this point, but sometimes we are prone to exhibit the interesting things of our churchmanship and fail to treasure the valuable things of faith. I am forever touched by the fact that sometimes churches get so interested in being clever they forget to strive to be compassionate. Such compassion is after all the measure of our authenticity.

Chapter Two

The Willington Simulcast had come. Sam barely got back from taking the chocolate-covered peanuts to old Kate and tried to listen as she sucked the chocolate off. She took so long at that, Sam barely got to the simulcast on time. The projectors whirred. The audio system popped. And Sam was most ready to begin the whole affair when . . .

Whammo!

In came a gentleman in a seventeenth-century English parson's costume. At first Sam thought it was someone from the church's clown ministry. Still he wore neither grease paint nor floppy shoes. Sam smiled. You just never knew who you were going to meet at a simulcast. It must be someone from the Christian Drama Club Convention who probably had a booth in the exhibit section underneath the auditorium.*

"Hi! I'm Sam!" said Sam.

"I know thee. Thou art good at it too!" said the man. The English accent seemed well done even for a crank.

"And you *are?*"

"I *are* Baxter," said the man in costume.

"Baxter!" said Sam. "Have you been making my hospital calls?"

"Well, somebody has to do it!" said Baxter.

"Don't tell me. Let me guess. You're part of the new evangelical protest against Halloween. When you're not making hospital calls, you come here to pass out anti-Harry Potter tracts?"

*Our culture is marked by a kind of Dow Jones Calvinism. Churches—and for that matter, pastors—are evaluated on their size or the size of their dreams and visions. Bigger is always seen as better. Why is bigger better? Because bigger is how we rate ourselves. One megachurch pastor puts it this way: "I typically plan my preaching schedule around our attendance patterns. From day one I have asked our staff to count every person who comes to our worship services. We counted when we had 150 people, and we count now that we have more than 15,000. Why is counting so important? We don't count so that we can pat ourselves on the back about our growth. We count so that we can build data on church attendance."[40]

I am glad this pastor doesn't count just to feed his ego, but even counting to keep attendance records seems less noble than getting to know people so you can meet their pastoral care needs.

†A recent article (1999) entitled "The Money Is Coming In but the People Are Going Out" was based on a survey of 604 senior pastors in the USA. It laments the large numbers of people leaving the church.[41] Most often when people do leave the church they are leaving because they feel the church failed to minister to them in a time of need. Yet pastors are often more stimulated to make their church grow than to care for its members in their needy times. No one ever gets his or her picture in an evangelical magazine simply because they visited the sick.

Baxter smiled and shook his head no.

"Well, then why this costume? Not that it's not well done, but why? Are you with the British Christian Clowns with Clowns International?" asked Sam.

"I'm not with any organization," Baxter answered.

"I'm pastor of a church and . . ."

"You want it to get bigger. Right?"

"Yes."

"Because bigger is better?"

"Better than smaller."*

"Really! You don't seem to have time to get to the hospital with your own small congregation. Why would you want it bigger?"

"I'll have you know, Baxter, our church is fully zonified!"

A seminar delegate just ahead of Sam turned toward him and said, "Hey, man, who are you talking to?"

"To Baxter . . ." said Sam, turning back toward the English gentleman.

He was gone!

Good! thought Sam. Nonetheless, the momentary distraction had only served to help Sam forget about the huge identity crisis at the center of his life. He just couldn't get over his feeling that he was a failure. He hated for the simulcast to begin because he knew his zonal care program was sick and maybe dying. He was a miniplayer in a megachurch world. Sam's feelings of failure were as regular as the arrival of *Church Growth* magazine. Every issue further convinced him that he was none too important in the world when compared with the megapeople who ran the seminars on how to do megathings. Pastoral care was never one of the "big things" by which a pastor might approve the purpose of his or her life.† There were the little people and the big people.

*This concept of anonymity is culturally related to the wider doctrine of privacy. It is this doctrine of megachurch that may stand too much in the way of traditional ecclesiology, particularly as regards pastoral care. While the megachurch goer may turn from being publicly recognized in worship, when things go wrong in those lives they do indeed turn with more of a need to be recognized because they are in a time of need. Park Brook Paul may use his anonymity to avoid a church visitor's house call or being called on to come forward in a church service during a time of public invitation, but he will desire less anonymity when he is admitted to the hospital. Still pastoral care mandates our knowing people so we can serve them in their time of need. The church goer's "right to privacy" also stands quite opposite to the idea of public confession of the lordship of Christ. One wonders if the current tendency toward anonymity can only end in a quiet and unacknowledged dismantling of the faith.

Churches—and pastors—were either *mini* or *mega,* and *mini* was Sam's prefix, but oh how he longed to be *mega!*

A part of Sam's problem was that he couldn't think of how to label his niche in the market. "Do you want to know who takes care of sick people at Park Brook?" blared the twenty-foot Willington from the simulcast screen. "Park Brook Paul, that's who." Will Willington, after doing his local church demographics, had labeled his typical congregational adherent as Park Brook Paul. Park Brook Paul was typically postmodern. He didn't want to be known; he wanted to go to a large church but hide out in the masses of theater seats full of thousands of others refugees from recognition.

No name tags. No "shake-a-little-hand-shake-the-hand-next-to-you," which could be sung by the rowdy and unrefined to the tune of "London Bridge" or "Puff the Magic Dragon," or for the truly inventive, "Ghost Riders in the Sky." The problem with the Ghost Riders tune was the abrasive yippee kai oh, yippee kai yay that came at the end of the phrase. It didn't bother the more athletic churches, but some found it offensive. But neither Park Brook Paul nor his wife, Park Brook Polly, wanted to sign visitors' cards or be asked to stand up and be introduced. They never signed visitors' cards and they sure didn't want to sing "Just As I Am," like the Baptists did. Back when Sam was truly mini, he used to give an invitation, but he had stopped it when a megachurch acquaintance of his asked him what you got when you crossed a Baptist preacher with a cell phone. Sam knew: it was an *altar call.*

Just the joke made him feel so ashamed, so old-fashioned, so John Wesley or Billy Sunday. Sam had done all these low-class, nonentrepreneurial things. But now he wanted to find some sort of clever way to designate his own members. He had thought of Amos Anonymous and Unknown Eunice or Hideaway Harry.

Sam may be confusing "vision" and "image." So many of the church growth books that one sees in Christian bookstores may be about image. Image is how we want to look when we have arrived on our pedestal of success. Vision, on the other hand, is what God has given us to do. But a simulcast is not necessarily the best place to discover the vision that God has for you. "You can't see a vision," says John Haggai, "when the artificial light of the Broadways, the Rialtos, and the commercial offices of the world blind your eyes . . . you are more likely to discern a vision in the cloistered halls of solitude than in the screaming jostle of the metropolitan concrete jungle. Perhaps in the cathedral of the trees, under the silence of the stars, or by the moaning sea, you'll be most likely to see that true light and hear the still, small voice."[42]

Pursuing our theme, no image attends the harder work of pastoral care. Yet oddly, after many years in a single congregation, the compliments of the hurting were always given to me for my care for their family in the hard times of life rather than for the fact that I had actually made the church grow.

It was these very driving issues that caused Sam to attend the Successful Pastor's Institute. He was trying to think better of himself. One of the big megamen had clearly said, "Hang around your heroes if you want to be heroic." When Sam was in seminary Jesus was his biggest hero, but Jesus didn't seem to be coming up all that often in the simulcasts. Even Park Brook Paul and Park Brook Polly didn't seem to have much interest in Jesus. But Jesus should be preached in such a way that Park Brook Paul couldn't tell you were doing it. Willington always said things like, "You can succeed best if you rely on the J-factor." Some people knew what the J-factor was but wouldn't tell others who were squeamish about having it said out loud. They liked success-oriented sermons and sermons on "how to" do this or that.

But the most remarkable thing about Park Brook Paul and Polly was that they never got sick—never needed pastoral care. They just went to church, smiled, listened, and went home and bragged to everyone they met about how large their church was. Now this was Sam's kind of church. No sickness, no hard times, just "happy to be here."

Still he was uneasy. His people did get sick, drat it all. Plus he knew he said "Jesus" far too often in his sermons. He felt that in spite of being a warm and informational preacher, his life was somehow on hold. It was mostly all those books that informed him on how to have a growing church that intimidated him. He felt ashamed when anyone asked him if he had read *Church Growth and the Grin of God*. Or, had he seen the video series *Getting Wide, Getting with It, Getting Wild?* *

He knew his problem. As Biff Wheeler had told him, he was only pastoring his church. He was merely leading his church to go deeper with God. What a shallow notion! Biff had told him a thousand times, "Nobody wants a deeper-with-God church, man.

*Robert Schuller was the first pastor I ever heard claim that he had polled his neighborhood to find out what people wanted in a church with the specific intention of giving them just that. But this has become the market-driven ploy of the contemporary beltway church. The church has too infrequently stopped to ask themselves, "Are we called to give them what they want, or is something more involved in the whole idea of ministry?" Would something have been lost if Jeremiah had determined to give Zedekiah what he wanted in a national prophet? Would God have smiled down on John the Baptist for saying, "I must try to be more of what Herodias would like in a man of God"? When it is all said and done, the reason we should not attempt to give people what they want in a church is that God wants so much more for them than they can imagine wanting for themselves.

†There is an assumption that only preaching matters in the pursuit of a calling. Not so. Long ago, W. E. Sangster wrote, "What a sad folly it is that has led ministers in many generations to see some innate controversy between preaching and pastoral work. To make an either/or of this double and related task is surely a suggestion of the devil. A man in any normal ministerial situation, tempted to put the emphasis on one of these tasks to the exclusion of the other, might well listen to his Master's word: 'This ought ye to have done and not to leave the other undone.'"[43]

‡Warren Bennis offered two laws of pseudodynamics. Law 1, he said, states that routine work drives out nonroutine work and smothers all creative planning. The second law states, "The trivial always replaces the grand."[44] Sam has come to see pastoral care as trivial and the little fly in the huge tub of ointment. How much better it would be to believe and serve both values at once.

Don't you read Barnie George? People want more activities. They want food courts, gyms, softball leagues, ski retreats, concerts. You know, the essential stuff."

Poll your neighborhood. Find out what people want in a church, then go build what they want.* Build a better mouse-trap—or sheepfold—and the world will beat a path to your neo-Gothic door. Why are you always refusing to steer your congregation toward Searcher Significance. You're trying too hard to meet needs. You've got to focus, Sam. Don't worry when people get sick. Ninety-seven percent of them get well again. Had not William Willington, the pastor of Newark's Park Brook Community Church, made it clear that every pastor needed to set aside the busy work and get searcher intensive? Pastor Willington had grown a church from one little, small-time, sniveling telemarketing survey to just under the size of the Third Reich in only twenty-one years.

Sometimes Sam felt so ashamed he was spending so much time with pastoral care. It was leaving him nonconversational around the coffee urns at pastors' breakfasts. While others slapped one another on the back and talked about their searcher intensive indices and how big their churches were, Sam mostly ate donuts in the dark corners, far from the bragging crowd. Preachers, it seemed to him, talked only about either their last game of golf or their next seminar. These were the activities of successful church-men. Biff Wheeler only had two pictures in his study. One was of Jesus, the other of Tiger Woods. Underneath these icons a callig-raphied sign read, "Did either of these men become great reading books on pastoral care?"[†]

Sam felt it was right for him to be attending the simulcast. He suddenly felt that to really please God, he should be right where he was—downlinking things off satellites and showing the tapes later of this Vivant Victory Simulcast to his entire church.[‡]

*Psychologists have pointed out the correlation between success and personal appearance and deportment. There was an old song that whined, "Short people have no reason to live." Of course, it's not only politically incorrect; it's also just plain false. Still church growth pastors are by and large "good looking." However there was an Elizabethan word that outdid it all. The word was *beautiful*. The King James Bible says of David that he was "beautiful." "David must have been one whose inner life rendered him beautiful. What is it that makes leaders *beautiful?* . . . Beautiful people are others-centered . . . . Beautiful then is often defined as being lost in a cause that is larger than ourselves. Further, inner beauty is enhanced when our own glory is unimportant."[45] I think, in considering such a definition of "beautiful" and "movie star," one realizes the two words are oxymorons, which could never stand in the same honest definition.

†I actually heard of a church that did this. A church in Texas has McDonald's in their food court and is affectionately called *McChurch* by some who attend there. During the "bus craze daze" of church growth, churches often gave prizes to children who rode buses. The point is that the marketing culture has exported the spirit of promotion right into the church. Even when churches don't promote in these supersales ways, they may tend to promote the various facets of their programs in more acceptable ways. Most large churches have some Christianized forms of "weight watchers," travel clubs, etc. None of these things are bad and may actually draw a great many people in to hear the gospel, but the point is that we learned none of these things from the Bible or in church history. It's just become the way we think. Ed Young Jr. says, "I often use a subtle but invaluable method of vision casting. During the announcements I might say, 'We're having a tennis clinic on Saturday. It's going to be a lot of fun and a great way to reach people, so bring your friends.' That simple statement affirms the reaching-out part of our vision and encourages members to evangelize."[46]

Let us recall the words of Erwin McManus: "We both expect and demand to be treated like consumers. 'If you want my patronage, you had better cater to my needs.' This type of ideology has become a reality for the church. In both traditional and contemporary churches, the member became the customer to whom the church was tailored."[47]

The odd thing about this view of member as consumer is that few see anything odd about it.

Sam's face broke into a wide smile.

Willington was on the screen. "You must be F. O.," said Willington, "Future Oriented—*carpé mañana.*" Oh, was this glorious!

"God help me be F. O.!" said Sam half aloud. The man ahead of him who had shushed him when he talked to Baxter turned and looked at him again. He then turned and faced the front of the auditorium again, but even as he did so, he pointed his index finger at the side of his head and made a little spiraling gesture that spelled "wacko!" for Sam. Then he looked around hurriedly to see if anyone else was within earshot. Fortunately there was not. Sam vowed to quit talking to himself.

Sam looked at his folder. He stared at the picture of Willington. It was an eight-by-ten and professionally produced. He looked like a movie star.* He lifted his eyes from the picture of the church growth god to focus on the projected Willington, glistening with information on the huge simulcast screen. Willington turned the program over to a Bible Belt mega Baptist pastor who began to speak just as Will Willington left the camera.

This pastor was well dressed. He was telling the simulcast audience that he had discovered that he could baptize more children by getting creative. The church, he said, had just refurbished an old fire truck, fitting the truck's ladder section with a fiberglass baptistry. As each "newly saved" preschooler went into the water with Jesus, the sirens went off and the cherry pickers flashed. This mega Baptist pastor felt it was definitely an improvement over the trinitarian formula for the little ones.† "Little children sometimes find baptism a little frightening," he said, "and back away from it. But they all like fire trucks. So we decided to contemporize and put a little more pizzazz into the Paraclete."

That particular pastor didn't bother Sam as much as the next megaman whose church food court had just begun to

*If this seems far out, remember that you can buy "Testamint" to sweeten your breath at some Christian bookstores and Christian tea bags with Scriptures printed on the paper tabs that read more secularly "Lipton's" in supermarkets. The art of Thomas Kinkade has many bizarre marketing ploys within the Christian marketplace. And all best-sellers have spin-off titles such as *Left Behind for* _____, and *The Prayer of Jabez for the* _____. The chicken-soup-for-the-soul marketers have taught the church that there's gold in "them thar hills." There can be little doubt the Christian is consumer and churches have joined with marketing firms to keep the image alive.

†Many of the causes to which Christian advocates commit themselves are no doubt most worthy. The problem may be that in many cases the passions that drive these advocates may displace their authentic place in the community's service. J. Stephen Muse wisely counsels us: "There is a saying among monks that 'if you go into the desert without being called by God, you will go mad.' Another way of saying this is, 'If you lose an authentic sense of ministry with a community, you will almost certainly develop an addiction.' Passions will take root in the place of the heart where the Spirit is supposed to dwell. The Eastern Orthodox Christian tradition defines as evil anything that is not in communion with God."[48]

serve triangular bagels called trinitarts, a great low-fat wit-
nessing snack.* It was too much. Sam needed a little air. So
he popped a couple of Testamints into his mouth and left the
auditorium and went outside where he could think over some
of the new methodologies he was hearing about. As he left the
church, Sam fought his way through one throng of women
carrying "Down with Harry Potter" signs. He then elbowed his
way through a picket line carrying "Gays Are Your Christian
Brothers and Sisters Too" signs. The third ring out were the
C-MADD (Christian Mothers Against Drunk Driving) moms.
The Christians-will-go-through-the-tribulation group held the
pavement nearest the parking lot. Sam could see that the various
political pressure groups were "ministries" that always seemed
to upstage pastoral care as much as the church growth groups.
Sam studied their signs from the back and wondered if any of
them helped make the churches' hospital visits.†

Sam was at last in his car driving away from the massive worship center of Beltway Community Church. Oh, it felt good to be
outside. Maybe he'd go have a burger. Maybe he'd have a mega-
burger and biggie-size it. Yes. Thank you, Lord, for fat people
who like grease and salt and things McEvil. Sam retreated into his
one great war against his poor self-image. Eat! Fast! Park Brook
Paul would be there, and Polly too. They'd be eating the same
kind of fluff they did on Sunday. Don't worry about nutrition.
Just eat. Fluff yourself up. Feel good!

After the burger Sam decided to make a few hospital calls.
Immediately he felt guilty. What would Willington do? Well, he
would not make hospital calls! Will had zonified. Sam suddenly
wondered why people in the megachurches never seemed to get
sick. The simulcasts never said so. Did they die? It seemed not.
The hordes who swarmed into megachurches only lived to go

*My suspicion is that the wounded abound in megachurches, but that finding authentic help may be obscured by the numbers business. Continually counting and measuring obscures deeper needs that may go unnoticed, buried under hype. J. Stephen Muse writes, "Those who most deeply understand the suffering of others have themselves been deeply wounded and worked their way through their hurt by relying on the grace of God. Problems arise when the position of helper or minister is used to heal one's own wounds by segregating oneself from those who need ministry themselves."[49]

to church and be counted and remain anonymous. No needs, no problems, just attend.* They were always pretty and young and all one middle-class color. *It was so simple,* thought Sam as he climbed in his car to go to the hospital. It was getting toward late and the fall sun had slipped under the horizon, thoughtfully making it easier to run the projectors inside the auditorium from which Sam was happy to be taking a short reprieve.

He drove. His mind was on idle. He was happy not to be thinking just how unhappy he was. He was having a bad case of McD, minichurch depression. He smiled as a car passed him with a dimly illuminated bumper sticker that read, "I'm having a better time since I've given up all hope." Sam smiled. To think about things you don't want to think about is the pits. Thinking was hard work. Hope was even harder. But biggie-sizing was still just an amazing thirty-nine cents. "Thank you, Jesus. Life is good," said Sam as he motored farther and farther away from the conference center.

Life sometimes turns on a dime, and to a man who lived on the small coinage of life, a dime held turning room. Sam was on the beltway after a grueling evening of emergencies. He marveled that people often picked the most inconvenient times to get sick or married or die. But thoughtless as they were, people seemed to be all-important to God. It was for this reason that Sam had stayed extra late at the hospital. So he knew he would be extra late getting home, and he hated getting home late.

He would have gone on driving and lamenting over his busy schedule when a dark hulk of steel loomed up unlit in his headlight. It looked like someone had just built a dark steel fortress in the middle of the highway. Sam cried out a little as he slammed on his brakes. His no-skid brakes argued with the damp pavement and began to do what they were not supposed to do—slide. Sam's car skidded up to the crinkled metal remains of a semi truck that had

*The use of the accident in the narrative is my way of enforcing the fact that most of the things that take the pastor's time are vast and overwhelming situations of pastoral care. They swoop down at once upon us and take the center of all we do until the last outreach of their need has been satisfied. It is true that our work is our interruptions; nonetheless, these interruptions are devastating to all other plans we may be pursuing when they fall upon us. Still, these are the holes in the human landscape that must be patched by God, and we must be faithful to human need as it arises, when it arises, or we sacrifice something very beautiful for the sake of pseudo-progress. One only has to look at how Jesus, bent on his program of world redemption, could be interrupted by pressing human concerns that required his full attention and ministry. No wonder E. M. Bounds wrote long ago, "Disciples of Jesus! You are called to be like your Lord in priestly intercession! When will we awaken to the glory of our destiny to pray to God . . . ? When will we shake off the sloth that clothes itself in humility and yield ourselves wholly to God's Spirit, that he might fill our wills with light and power to know, to take, and to possess everything that our God is waiting to give?"[50] I have discovered that most of all which God is waiting to give me comes not in the reading of books or how-to manuals. Rather, it all comes in the demand—sometimes the all-consuming heavy demand—of the desperate cry for pastoral care.

crashed into an interstate bridge abutment. The wreckage of the huge truck was dark, and yet it was clear to Sam that the accident had just occurred. In fact, he faced the fear he had always dreaded: being the very first person upon the scene of a serious accident.*

Before Sam even began the ominous walk toward the front of the wreckage, he did instinctively what had to be done. He used his cell phone to call 911 and report the accident. He struggled in the darkness to make clear to the person at the station desk exactly where he was on the beltway. It was near the hospital exit in the northbound lane. The location seemed adequate. Sam could tell the answering officer nothing about the extent of the damage or what had caused the wreck, or if there was any life in danger.

Once the call was concluded, Sam left his car running with the headlights trained on the foreboding pile of steel before him. He also left his car's flashers strobing their red and amber warning to anyone approaching from the rear. He took his small and weak-beamed flashlight from the glove box and moved cautiously around the dark wreckage. At the front of the truck he was horrified to see that the heavy trailer had hurtled forward upon impact and crushed the cab, almost beyond recognition. The hapless driver was pinned in between the bent steel at the back of the cabin and shoved forward over the steering wheel so that his upper torso was bent almost directly above the dashboard. At first glance the driver appeared to be fine. He was smiling. Even in his horribly cramped posture he told Sam almost cheerfully that he was "all right," and would be glad when the crew arrived to get him out of the crunch of steel. "I fell asleep, I guess. Man, is my company gonna be . . . I'm gonna lose my job over this one."

Sam used the thin, weak beam of his flashlight to trace down the back of the truck's seat. To his horror Sam could tell that there was a great deal of blood in the lower part of the cab, and that where his

*I actually had a Christian trucker friend who died in such a manner. The circumstances were vastly different than this because the actual instance on which this is based happened to a man who did not fall asleep driving. And above all, he was a Christian. Still, his dying became a wonderfully important, weeklong interruption in my life as pastor of a growing church. I can remember after all such incidents, which required extensive seasons of pastoral care, that I had the odd sensation of returning from the demanding world at hand to resume my usual life as a church growth pastor. I never resented these interrupting crises. They contained and always will contain the momentary demand of God. If Jesus' interruptions were cherished by the Son of God, bent on such a mission as he was, surely no servant is greater than his Lord.

lower torso would have been there were white fragments of bones
sticking through the driver's horribly mangled flesh. Sam could tell
that the lower half of the driver's body had been all but amputated
from the upper half by a steel girder in what had been the back of the
cab. The driver was in more serious shape than he knew.

Sam moved the light back to the driver's face. He knew the
man had no idea of the trouble he was in. He knew the moment
when the police and wrecker crews arrived they would also see the
horrible conundrum. To liberate the man would be to kill him.
When the sealing pressure was removed from his crushed body,
Sam knew he would die. The very moment that the steel loosed
its clammy fingers from his lower abdomen—the horrible instant
that the metal was pried away—the rush of blood now sealed in
this vise of steel would flood downward, ending the man's life.[*]

The driver could tell by looking at Sam's face that things were
not well.

"Am I going to live, sir?" he asked.

"I'm sorry, partner," said Sam wishing he had picked another
word, wishing there was some better word. "Things don't look
so good from here. When the pressure against your body is
released . . ." Sam stopped.

The driver understood.

"Sir," the driver said with surprising volume and strength, "can
you reach my wallet? It's in my left hip pocket." Sam wiped away
the dark blood and reached into his pocket and found the wallet.
He drew it out, wiped the blood from it as best he could, and climb-
ing higher in the wreckage of the rig, extended it toward him.

"Open it," said the driver. Sam obeyed. An inner section of
photos fell open.

"Hold your light right there . . . on that photo," said the driver.
Once again Sam obeyed.

*In *All's Quiet on the Western Front,* I am touched by the two dying soldiers from opposing armies who happen to fall into the same foxhole. In their dying moments they no longer rehearsed the animosities that taught them to kill each other simply for being from different countries. Instead they show each other the photographs of their families drawn from their wallets. Above their inabilities to speak each other's languages, the photographs of their wives set at a distance their preclusion to hate or kill.

The truck driver has brought to Sam's attention the intersection of such worlds. These who never knew each other must focus on the intimate worlds, previously unknown, but brought to light in a tragedy. I never got over this feeling as a pastor. I was walking into the Holy of Holies of family life. In these sanctuaries of desperation, nothing that I thought important from church manuals was of ultimate significance. Only my walk with Christ awakened me to the need of pastoral care and gave me the right to enter these desperate temples of need.

†T. S. Eliot once said, "I had far rather walk, as I do, in daily terror of eternity, than feel this was only a children's game in which all the contestants would get equally worthless prizes in the end."[51] This terror of eternity is the edgy work of invading peoples' lives at their invitation. It is carrying the important incarnation of peace into their homes because we ourselves have become his incarnation. These are the credentials of pastoral care, Jesus' life in us.

"That's my wife," the man said.*

"She's a beautiful woman," Sam said.

"Sir, what's your line of work?" The question stopped Sam. It seemed so blatantly unimportant in such a desperate time.

"I'm the pastor of a church."

"Oh, thank God. You're just the one who should be here. God must be good to work it all out like this."

Sam wondered how the man could find anything of God in the tons of dark wreckage that was taking his life.

"Try not to talk. Save your strength. Maybe we can get your wife here. Do you live near here? Are you a local driver?" Sam felt guilty for telling the man to save his strength and then promptly asking him such demanding questions.

"Yes, not a mile from here. I was almost home when . . . ." An unseen chill caused the driver to shudder as though he was feeling the approaching demon of death.

"Sir, would you call my wife? The address is here on my driver's license. Would you tell her I love her. Just this afternoon, over the phone, we had a terrible fight. It's most important that she know that I love her. Tell her I beg her forgiveness for the way I treated her, for the things I said."†

"Of course," said Sam. Even as he answered he heard the scream of the approaching sirens. He knew that, before long, the truck would become a swarm of activity. He would then be more in the way than of any real help.

"Pastor, I've not been the best of men. I've got a lot of fences to mend with God, I'm afraid. Could you give me a prayer, Reverend? Tell God I'm sorry I've too often left him out of the mess I've made of my life. Tell him I'm on the way. And Reverend, would you hold that picture where I can see it, and would you just hold my hand while you pray? Then after the prayer, I want you

61

*Christopher Lasch said that New Age spirituality was rooted in narcissism.[52] It is the purest moment of pastoral care that our own name seems, even to us, obscene, in lieu of the all-sufficiency of Christ, and what he wants to get done in such a needy moment and in such a needy place.

†I have many times found myself in the midst of rather mundane things that go with the life of a caregiver. I confess that I never felt adequate, like serving God by going to court with a needy family or helping a new widow fill out the paperwork for Social Security benefits. I never felt qualified, and that was because I wasn't. Still the counsel of God is faithful even in the face of the boring "aspiritual" requirements of pastoral care. The Holy Spirit can become the counselor in all things. Dorotheos of Gaza wrote, "Do not ponder what you should do if you have no one to ask. If anyone really in truth desires the will of God with all his heart, God never leaves him to himself but always guides him according to his will. If a man really set his heart upon the will of God, God will enlighten a little child to tell that man what the will of God is."[53] Is it possible that all things might be done improperly yet still be in order? I suppose it is, but in all the instances of "legalistic necessities" in which the days forced me to help, I was never in trouble for offering a hand. Caregivers should be careful to consult with others wiser than they are and refer some to professionals more qualified than they are to be sure they are offering the most useful and correct help, however.

to take the picture to my wife, Frances. Tell her you got it talking to me, and tell her that I died in grace."

Sam took the driver's left hand. The right one disappeared into wreckage on the other side of his body. "I'm Sam," he said awkwardly. For the life of him it needed to be said, and yet upon his life he couldn't think of a single reason why his name was important.*

"I'm Frank—Frank Trakowsky. My wife's name is Frances," said the driver.

Sam clamped his eyes shut and began. "Lord, Frank wants you to know he's sorry for leaving you out of his life. He's on the way, Lord. Greet him gently. And, Lord, help Frances to know how much he loved her. . . ."

Sam felt Frank's fingers go limp. Sam knew he was gone. He took the picture of the Trakowskys out of the trucker's wallet and then climbed down from the cab. About the time he prepared to leave, the scene of the accident began to get busy.

Sam memorized the address on the license, just as the police arrived. Sam handed the officer in charge the wallet. Two other squad cars were pulling up as Sam turned to leave.

"Were you a witness to this accident?" asked the officer. "He appears to have dozed off and ran full speed into this bridge abutment. There are no skid marks. It must have been that. A single vehicle accident."†

"It was a single vehicle accident. He told me he just fell asleep," said Sam. "I happened to be the first to come along. I did talk to him a little before he died. His name was Frank." Sam pulled one of his business cards from his shirt pocket and handed it to the officer as he walked away. "Call me, if I can be of any help whatever."

When Sam returned home that night his head was swimming with the odd juxtaposition of a dying trucker and a church growth conference. He determined that on the morrow he would

*Fools rush in where angels fear to tread. It is always daunting to step into the middle of tragedy and to try and help. Even the finest of counselors must be humble enough to feel a sense of interference. Yet, as we have said, pastoral care is edgy work, and there are no manuals written to define the limits of propriety. We who are pastors are in love with the world, and we have work to do. This is our commission as incarnations of the Christ who cares. People don't need to see us, but they do need to see him. Why? Because it is not only the giver of pastoral care who is confused and overwhelmed by the crisis; those who have been bludgeoned by the crisis are also overwhelmed. Naturally we feel reluctant to enter the fray which no one understands. In another context Walter Brueggemann said it is all like coming into new circumstances and being forced to live in a "new home. People need pastoral care to help in relinquishing a home that is gone, and more help to enter their new home which is so new that it feels dangerously threatening and deeply alien."[54] Every crisis requires a pastor to walk into a home or situation which is in a sense cross-cultural. Yet the very foreign feel of the situation calls us to a new dependency on Christ. Our comfort level and our importance vary inversely in these terrifying situations.

†Crises are meant to give our present dreams meaning and not to destroy them. We are called to enter the world of pastoral care and serve as though we are visiting on the planet. But our ordinary work of building the kingdom and making Christ a visible presence in evangelism and church growth are always to remain near at hand. The ordinary days of our church leadership and the crises must have one thing in common: the definite sense that we are in the will of God, whichever world we call home. Paul Little wrote, "When problem and stresses arrive, they do not indicate we are out of God's will. There are times when we take a step of obedience . . . and the bottom falls out of everything. Then only our confidence that we were in the will of God keeps us going."[55]

go and see Frances Trakowsky. The police by that time would have been there, and she would have had some time to seek the counsel of her closer friends. He knew inwardly he was most reluctant to make the call.* He wasn't even sure how he would begin the conversation. But he had made the promise, and he must do what he had promised.

Once at home, Sam poured himself a glass of milk and tried to think through the odd proceedings of the evening. He wanted his church to grow just like Will Willington's. And he wasn't even opposed to instituting his methods. But when the image of the dying trucker came to mind, somehow the whole church growth seminar seemed oddly egoistic and unworthy. It seemed glitzy and unimportant in lieu of the life-shattering events facing a dead trucker's widow.

He sat down in his easy chair, stretched out as far as he could, and loosened his shirt. He shook his head as though the violence of the motion would erase the odd jumble of thoughts in his mind. It was then that he caught sight of the book that he had been reading earlier that day. It was the leading book on church growth, entitled *The Neon Yahweh,* which was subtitled: *Is Your God Too Biblical?* It was the year's number-one church growth book on how to get God out of the burning bush and into the laser age. But what of that poor trucker? How could Sam even think of engineering church growth in the face of such an unanswerable crisis.†

Sam had to play the man—the man of God. It was time to put away Will Willington and try to get in touch with Jesus! All the church growth manuals said that God hated sniveling little churches. God was big, like an Anaheim parking lot; and when the need was less intense, Sam wanted to be big. But Frances Trakowsky hadn't read any church growth literature, and she needed something far more basic than a megamanual.

*Old-line denominationalists are highly critical of the huge numbers game that accompanies megachurch reputation. Those who are actually a part of megachurches make it clear that the old-line denominations, being captive to their own "death wish," have nothing solid to criticize about. But Rick Warren's emphasis on church health seems to arrive at the best resolution of the argument. Christian Schwarz of the Institute for Natural Church Development says that it is high time that the church growth field focuses on church health instead of numbers. Schwarz rejects the drive for bigger numbers and says churches should be allowed to grow naturally without pushing numbers at the congregation.[56]

He fell asleep in his easy chair with the last chapter of *The Neon Yahweh* opened flat against his chest. The chapter was entitled "Uplifting Your Church, Downlinking Your Vision." The warmth of the room left him dozing, oozing warmly in and out of consciousness. His easy chair was mysteriously transformed into a first-class seat on an important airliner. He could see through the mists that he was wearing a Tommy Bahama shirt, opened generously to reveal his bronze physique. No clerical collar. He was Pastor-Contempo. He was carrying a burgundy leather copy of the Swingin' English Bible—the SEB. No briefcase. Just a conference folio stamped with gold, "The Neon Yahweh Church Growth Seminar." He found himself singing, "Jehovah Jireh, Yeah, Yeah, Yeah!" to his fellow passengers in first class.*

There was a sudden flash of incandescence and a loud pop. It was the crack of a tungsten filament. A lightbulb had blown in his reading lamp, leaving the room dimly lit. Sam hated it when a lightbulb exploded and then just quit. It seemed so like a revival.

"Would you have preferred it fizzled, like your searcher intensive index," said a very crisp British voice, calling Sam to instant awareness.

The strange voice shook Sam alert and left him trembling. Someone was in the room with him. He stared into the smoky darkness that followed the pop of the lightbulb.

"Who's there?"

"Baxter, old chap. Baxter the Poltergeist."

"Poltergeist!" said Sam, "but you're the guy who came to the simulcast for a few minutes earlier today."

"Yes, old chap, I am. I decided not to stay too long. Not much of value going on. A lot of nonsense about trying to build churches into monsters that no one could effectively pastor." The ghost was highly critical and very English about it.

*Most pastoral care in any century has had to fight for its right to be in the face of the various millennial movements that have characterized the climate of the time. Premillennialism has nearly always been a corollary of church growth. Premillennial churches tend to grow faster than those with no opinion on the subject: "Randy Jarvis grew up and became Pastor Jarvis. He studied at a well-known dispensational seminary and became an expert in prophecy and end times. His sermons were powerful and his church grew and grew and grew."[57]

†As Baxter is surprised to find that churches grow in America, people in the next century will remember America only as a place where churches once grew but no more (See Philip Jenkins, *The Next Christendom*). One can only wonder if the abandonment of pastoral care in the attempt to get bigger is not a part of the equation that is causing Christianity's shift of power to South America, Africa, and the Pacific Rim. It is a question worth considering.

"Who let you in?" asked Sam as his terror began to fade into reason. He wondered what had happened to his Brinks monitoring system. "How did you get in without setting off the alarm?"

"I just showed the gatekeeper my pass and gave him your address and 'poof!' here I was right here in . . . . Excuse me, do you have the time?"

Sam looked at his watch. "Ten-fifteen," he replied.

"No, I don't mean the time of day. I'm talking calendars. I'm still on seventeenth-century standard. What year is it?"

"We just got started on the third millennium."

"So the Fifth Monarchists were wrong with all those second-coming Bible studies of theirs. I always thought they were. I kept trying to tell them King Louis was not the Antichrist, nor was the fleur-de-lis the mark of the beast.* But they all kept insisting that we were going to be left behind if we didn't see things their way! They kept saying that the Jews were going to rebuild the temple in Jerusalem. Have they rebuilt it yet?"

"Not yet," smiled Sam.

"Well, what do you know! I never could tell those people a thing. They always kept insisting that Jesus would be back before supper. But then what millennial movement ever preached Jesus was coming later?" Baxter the Ghost stopped and patted his whiskers thoughtfully with his hand. "These things amaze even me. Say, is this Bristol?"

"No," Sam said, somewhat bewildered. "This is America!"

"America! Then you're a colonialist! Can you actually grow churches in America?† Who would have ever thought things would progress this far. Did you people ever settle down and pay your taxes cheerfully and start drinking tea and flying the Union Jack again?"

"Excuse me, does your little drop-in have a point?" asked Sam.

*What Baxter observed in terms of pastoral care in his day was probably true of all days, including our own. Rick Ezell explains our culture in terms of its competitiveness and not its congenial brotherhood: "Today, many are advancing their careers, but few seem interested in building sound character. All too frequently, who we are is sacrificed upon the altar of ambition and worldly success . . . . People emphasize doing rather than being, accomplishment rather than character. Nothing is wrong with accomplishment, but who we are is more important than what we do. Many people . . . are so wrapped up in winning at a game or profession that they forget to win at life."[58]

"Well, the word up in our corner of eternity is that you have a bit of a bugaboo with pastoral care. I wrote a book on the subject back in the seventeenth century."

"Oh, so you're that Baxter! Richard Baxter! I read your book in seminary."

"Really, old man, what year?"

"You mean what year did I read your book?"

"Exactly."

"1992, I think," said Sam, trying to recall the very year.

"Amazing! You can still buy it all these centuries later. I'm glad it's still selling. To be honest, it didn't sell all that well at the time."

"I hate to burst your bubble . . ."

"My bubble? Is this a metaphor?"

"Skip it," said Sam. "The truth is, your book isn't doing all that well now, either."

Baxter looked a little crestfallen.

"Well, I'm not surprised. Pastoral care is always out of style with some in every age. Life has few perks for the small-church pastor doesn't it, Sam? Every good man of God's gotta do his own pastoral care!"

Sam nodded.

"Well, life in the seventeenth century was no picnic either. The Church of England was so corrupt. Every priest wanted power and influence. Nobody much was interested in pastoral care back then either, I can tell you. All of them were trying to become the dean of some great cathedral. There was a lot of foolish competition among pastors.* They should have known they couldn't all have their own cathedrals. There just weren't enough to go around. Well, the point is, nobody wanted to minister."

Sam smiled.

*Larry Christianson reminds us that all of the circumstances of our lives become the places where God can speak to us. If this be true, then the mundane organizational items in a pastor's life hold opportunities for God to speak to us as the grand arenas of need which sew up our lives to the exclusion of the ordinary programmable issues of pastoral care. But the truth is, all of it adds up to pastoral care. The issue is the pastoral caregiver must listen for the voice of the Spirit in all circumstances. "The Lord Jesus and the Holy Spirit communicate with us in and through the circumstances of our everyday lives. Their communication through circumstances can be quite clear, but it is indirect. They speak to us through the words of other people. They help us read the meaning of unfolding events. They quietly direct our thoughts and prayers until we come to a place where we recognize their purpose. They underscore the requirements of our station and calling in life."[59] I suppose, however, that most pastors feel occasionally as I did. Whenever I was helping a family in draconic crisis, I resented the trivial interference of churchy people with churchy problems. It took me years to realize that what seemed petty to me did not seem petty to everyone. All of it in one way or another was pastoral care.

†"Christianity has come to the point where we believe that there is no higher aspiration for the human soul than to be nice. We are producing a generation of men and women whose greatest virtue is that they don't offend anyone."[60]

‡What good pastoral care communication aims at is getting the words right, so the mood will be right, so we can arrive at an understanding of pastoral intimacy. This intimacy bespeaks a oneness between the caregiver and the care receiver. But this struggle to build warmth and oneness is hard to achieve. Chip Dodd says this intimacy is achieved whenever we live in "truthfulness, transparency, vulnerability, and responsibility."[61] But pastoral care must add at least one other highly significant virtue—tact. Not just tact. It must be a tact that bends over backward to be sure it is gracious enough that it could not possibly offend anyone.

The phone rang. Baxter, who had seen nothing unusual in terrifying Sam, looked terrified at the sound. "There are a lot of things you're going to have to get used to, Baxter. Pardon me while I answer the phone."

It was Earl Payton. He had such a lilt in his voice that Sam could only feel sure that Earl had fully forgiven him for the stoplight challenge and the nose-picking gesture. In addition to being a zonal compassion committee member, Earl was also the president of the men's ministries at the church. "Pastor," said Earl, "would you be able to read the prayer list at the fish fry on Thursday night?"*

"I'm sorry," answered Sam, "but I'm over at Beltway Community Church throughout the week, attending the Vivant Victory Successful Pastor Simulcast."

"Oh, the VVSPS?"

"Uh . . . yes," agreed Sam. He was surprised! Earl had the alphabet soup right. Never mind that Sam hated praying at fish fries.

"I don't know if you've heard this or not, but Emma Johnson is having a biopsy tomorrow," said Earl.

Sam couldn't think of what to say. "Too bad" seemed too little. "Oh?" was just right. He hated measuring his words as he did because he felt it reduced pastoral care to the grinning idiocy of being nice.†

"Well, she's been having some pains in her abdominal area."

"Abdominal?"

"It means 'in the stomach area,'" explained Earl. "The doctor says it could be lesions, could be a tumor, could be an ulcer."

Sam liked Earl's multiple choice. *Hmmn,* mused Sam: *a. lesions, b. tumor, c. an ulcer.* Trying to be nice, he said, "Well, let's pray that it's an ulcer."

"Why would you pray for Emma to have an ulcer?"

"Well, it's better than a lesion or tumor."‡

*Most of us live with a sense of toxic shame because we are caught up in an inability to feel like Jesus feels because we can't manage to love as God loves. Chip Dodd convicts me in the matter when he says, "Toxic shame entangles our hearts, rightly binding them up, leaving us unable to experience full life."[62] It is difficult to be a pastor and not love some members and relate to their needs more than other members. But unless we make an effort to pray honestly for our enemies, we are not only as bad off as the Pharisees; we are not at all like Jesus. This is the place where our inner feelings of shame become toxic because we are living in contradiction of the love of God.

"Oh ... well I guess so, but let's all just pray that it goes away."

Sam could see that Earl had the best option: none of the above. After Earl hung up, he made a note to see Emma when he visited the hospital the next afternoon.

"Somebody sick?" said Baxter, who had been kind enough to sit quietly while Sam was on the phone.

Sam replied, "Yeah, one of my members, not even one of my favorite members. What do you do, Baxter, when someone you don't even like gets sick? I almost wish it was someone I did like. While I hate to see my real supporters suffer, you feel more genuine when you pray for their recovery."*

Baxter the Ghost laughed out loud. "I knew an obnoxious Welshman—quite a gossip, infernal soul that he was. Anyway, he got the ague, and I was forced to pray for his recovery."

"Did he get well?"

"Yes ... blast it all! The bloke got well. Spoiled the church till the day he died. When he recovered he was just as obnoxious as ever, bringing his infernal plague of gossip back from the dead with him. I never minded raising the dead; it was just the obnoxious dead I hated to raise. That was always the problem I had with the Lord. He loves everybody, you know. No discretion with God. Thieves and bullies get the same affection as the saints. But when I agreed to ordination, I agreed to love everyone God loves. Hard bargaining with the Holy Spirit."

"Excuse me, how big was your church?" asked Sam.

"Big? What do you mean, old chap? About sixty by ninety feet, I guess."

"No, I don't want your square footage. I want your gate, your walk-ins, your crowd size, how many sheep you had in your Sunday morning fold."

*Richard Baxter, in describing the biblical ignorance of his day, certainly describes the biblical ignorance of ours. George Barna agrees that the megachurch has been no real savior in bringing America back to a better knowledge of the Scriptures: "As the church has abandoned the Bible, knowledge of scriptural content has declined, personal Bible reading has declined, the image of the Bible as sacred literature has declined, and the ability of people to comprehend biblical principles has declined. In fact, when it comes time to discuss what the church ought to be, biblical exhortations do not even enter the discussion."[63]

†"Every flock should have its own pastor, and every pastor his own flock. As every troop or company in a regiment of soldiers must have its own captain and other officers, and every soldier knows his own commander and colours, so it is with the will of God; every church should have its own pastor, and that all Christ's disciples should know their teachers that are over them in the Lord."[64]

‡Baxter was convinced that pastors should not have more members than they could care for: "O, happy Church of Christ, were the labourers but able and faithful, and proportioned in number to the number of souls; so that the pastors were so many, or the particular churches so small, that we might be able to take 'heed to all the flock.' . . . We must labour to be acquainted, not only with the persons, but with the state of all our people, with their inclinations and conversations . . . . Being thus acquainted with the flock, we must afterward take heed to them. One would imagine that every reasonable man would be satisfied of this, and that it would need no further proof. Doth not a careful shepherd look after every individual sheep?"[65]

"Well, what difference does that make? We never counted them. The room was mostly filled except during the plagues. But it never occurred to us to count them. Ours was an age when people were so mixed up doctrinally that it wouldn't matter how many came. There were so few who really believed the Bible, or even knew what it said, that if I had been the pastor at Westminster Abbey to a thousand, there wouldn't have been ten who knew who hanged Haman or who owned Onesimus.* We actually had people who believed epistles were the wives of apostles and that Balaam's ass was saddlebroke. We actually had people who wore the Holy Rood on leather thongs around their wrists to shorten their time in purgatory. Then they all wondered around asking what would Jesus do? Don't know why. None of them ever did it. It was a very wayward day."

"Still it sounds wonderful! No church growth clinics!"

"Church growth? You mean some insane pastors actually pray for their churches to get bigger? Have more people?"

"That's exactly what I mean. We've got churches that claim sixty thousand adherents."

"You mean like with one pastor?"

"Exactly!"

"What a bad notion. People should be able to know their pastor. Such knowledge is imperative for an effective ministry."[†]

"Well, I want a big church. I want to preach to . . . oh I don't know . . . sixty thousand . . . I can't imagine it, but that's what I want."

"Why man? Why would anyone want to be pastor of so preposterously large a church—sixty thousand! Why, that was the entire population of London in my time.[‡] No pastor should have more people than he can care for. Why, we must have had fifty cathedrals and churches. There was Saint Clemons, Saint Martins, Shoreditch, the Abbey, Old Bailey, Bowe, Saint Paul's . . ."

"Well, how big were they?"

*Os Guinness reminds us that style is the leading currency in modern society: "the main artery of American identity and belonging."[66] The arrival of the *form follows function* theory of architecture marks us as a people who know how to seat and amplify, but our buildings do not mark us as a people who know how to be creative. With the exception of Leith Anderson's Wooddale Church, virtually no extreme megachurch has come up with an architectural style that states any of its significant beliefs in God.

"Big? Why all this big stuff? Is that all you blokes want to talk about—big? When the great bells began to ring on Sunday . . ."

"Did the people in the neighborhood ever call in and complain about the noise?"

"Noise. No noise. Why, the bells swung all over the city, and it seemed like they were talking together. The children even had a little nursery rhyme to describe their conversation. They'd sing:

Oranges and Lemons, say the bells of Saint Clemons.
You owe me five farthings say the bells of Saint Martins.
When will you pay me say the bells of Old Bailey?
When I grow rich, say the bells of Shoreditch.
When will that be, say the bells of Stepney?
I do not know, say the great bells of Bowe.

Glorious were those bells! You should have heard them clean the air of frost on a misty October morning when you could see the breath of God waiting for the sun."

"Well," said Sam, "we don't have bells anymore; the neighbors complained. We keep our own boom boxes to provide noise. Now we build our buildings one story, low to the ground, no bells, no colored windows, no organs, just slides, guitars, and projectors."*

"Really. What do the sextons do?"

"No sextons, just ushers and tellers to count stuff."

"Count?"

"You know. People and money. Noses and nickels!"

Baxter scratched his head and began to fade into the gloom. Then the air swallowed his form. He was gone. The room was as quiet as it had been before he came. This unnerved Sam. The only thing worse than having a ghost in the manse was having a come-and-go ghost who started arguments he didn't stay to finish.

Sam had never told anyone about Sermoniel. Now he was talking to a ghost. He knew people in his congregation would think he

*Richard Baxter was beginning to have his effect on Sam. The individual work of pastoral care was paramount to those who needed it. Had not Baxter said, "We must be diligent in visiting the sick, and helping them to prepare for either a fruitful life or a happy death . . . . When time is almost gone, and they must now or never be reconciled to God, oh, how doth it concern them to redeem those hours and to lay hold on eternal life."[67]

was crazy if they knew. Baxter's odd appearance kept him up half the night. He didn't see him anymore, but he had the most awful notion that he still lingered in the dark categories of the manse ready to spring on him and bludgeon him dumb for attending a simulcast. Obviously, the ghost had no tolerance for the VVSPS.

It was the oddest day Sam could ever remember. He hated it, but he knew he would have to arrive at the simulcast a little late in the morning. He knew he first had to call on Frances Trakowsky. She needed him and he would have to go. He rebuked himself for thinking it was more important for him to see her than to attend the VVSPS.* He felt the very foundation of his desire to be mega was eroding under the constant tides of human need.

More important? What was he thinking? *Nothing was more important than succeeding.* He felt ashamed for even daring to think so small. He knew as long as pastoral care was so important to him, he would never succeed. Should he go and see Frances Trakowsky? Then there was Emma Johnson as well. Should he go see her? She had been such a pain all through his ministry. Maybe he could just pray for Emma while he was at the simulcast. But what of Mrs. Trakowsky? He prayed for insight, but the Lord answered not neither by the Urim or the Thummim. He had already paid his money to attend the simulcast. Should he skip even one session, just to do pastoral care? What a sniveling, petty notion. What would Will Willington do?

Chapter Three

The next morning, Sam tried to sort through the previous day's events. He knew the truck accident was real. He had the photo the trucker had given him. But he wondered if he really had held a conversation with the ghost of Richard Baxter. It was all a bit overwhelming; nonetheless, it stayed at the front of his tortured mind.

While he continued sifting the whole thing through his mind, his eyes wandered to the sofa where the British poltergeist had been sitting the night before. His eyes suddenly fell upon a little black book that was lying on one of the sofa cushions. Sam wondered how it had gotten there. The only possible explanation of it was that Baxter must have left it. When he picked it up, he could see it was full of notations, dates and appointments, and notes. The letters were English, but the old kind where final s's all looked like lowercase f's, and all the verbs ended in "est" or "eth." The pronouns, too, were all Elizabethan.

One notation was called *A prayer for Effie Hampton who hath the ague.* Another notation was for Thomas of Wales whose *gossip thou dost abhor, O Lord!* It was more poetic.

> Dear God of Earth and heath and moor
> Heal Tom of Wales who's kept indoor,
>
> Take him home to be with thee, and leave this world
> most bright and fair.

*There is no indication that Richard Baxter was the poet I'm portraying him to be. Blame this exaggeration solely on me.

†Baxter never saw the sermon as primary in pastoral care. He believed Christian compassion was the virtue that made the sermon work. "Alas, it is the common danger and calamity for the church to have unregenerate and inexperienced pastors, to have so many men become preachers before they are Christian."[68]

‡Kiddermaster was the name of Baxter's seventeenth-century parish. It is a sin to try to minister grace when you do not treasure it in your own personal and private inwardness: "Many a tailor goes in rags, that maketh costly clothes for others; and many a cook scarcely licks his fingers when he hath dressed for others the most costly dishes. Believe it brethren, God never saved any man for being a preacher, nor because he was an able preacher; but because he was a justified, sanctified man, and consequently faithful in his Master's work. Take heed, therefore, to yourselves first, that you be that which you persuade your hearers to be, and believe that which you persuade them to believe, and heartily entertain that Saviour whom you offer to them."[69]

§How indeed did we become more interested in counting people than redeeming them. George Hunter also wonders why and how we have forsaken our mission: "Not many churches are yet following Christ to reach the receptive New Barbarians who are all around us. That is tragic because deep down most of these people want to experience God's forgiveness and acceptance; they would like a second chance and a new life. The church has what they are looking for, but it is not offering it to them!"[70]

With him in heaven we'd be free, for thou wouldst
    have the blaggard there.
But if thou wouldst that he stay here, Then heal him
    Lord and end our cheer.[*]

Sam smiled. He kept on reading and working his way
through Baxter's old appointment book. He found one notation
that read:

The Sunday crowd hath disappeared I fear.
Could it be my lecturing hath rotted.
My sermons do seem cankered,
My homilies bespotted.[†]

But the notation that really captured his attention was one
that seemed more wrenching:

God, can I be counted faithful?
This world is such a hurting place.
So large the bleeding hereabout.
So small my bandages of grace.
Shall I of England fashion Galilee?
Christ shant in Kiddermaster be,
Unless he deigns to live in me.[‡]

There was something so mighty in Baxter's Ghost that Sam
was unable to shake the force of his concern for his world. He suddenly felt ashamed that all he wanted to do was to count people
and watch his church get bigger. He wondered how church had
ever become so oriented around such a narrow definition concerning how many people showed up for worship.[§] It suddenly
seemed as odd to Sam as it had to Baxter. Meditating upon the
odd discrepancy, he dressed for the day. Just before he walked out
the door he once more picked up Baxter's odd little journal from

*Even the sincere church and the sincere pastor have had trouble keeping everybody happy while they do the work of pastoral care. Whether or not Richard Baxter lamented congregational criticism, I don't know. But I do know that congregational criticism has grown rampant in our own day. No profession is more beleaguered than that of the pastor. Lloyd Rediger calls those who criticize the pastor incessantly *Clergy Killers*. He says their weapon of choice is conflict. "Conflict is normal in all relationships, but the conflict stirred up by clergy killers cannot be resolved through normal avenues. In most conflicts reasonable people can come to a compromise or resolve to disagree amicably. Clergy killers abuse or attack pastors, running them out of churches or the ministry. The main issue is control; over churches, individuals or anything else."[71] George Barna would agree with this: "Being a pastor these days may be the single, most thankless task in America. National surveys indicate that people are less likely to trust and to be influenced by clergy than used to be the case, and that pastors themselves are increasingly frustrated in ministry."[72]

his night stand. He read a few more pages from it. One notation jumped out at him.

> Five thousand ate the loaves and fishes, according to
>   Saint Matthew's tale,
> But several thousand whispered later that the bread
>   was somewhat stale.
> It's quite impossible to please
>   a cur that focuses on fleas.*

Sam read on through the difficult pages as far as he had time. He was especially touched by a passage that read:

> I never found thee much at home where thousands
>   mouthed some liturgy.
> I found thy presence more abundant where the needy
>   called to thee.
> It's rare indeed that masses
> Sing a song that passion knew.
> The whispered hymns of broken men
> Are anthems to the needy few.

Sam laid aside the book. He dressed himself in a kind of melancholy. He realized that the content of Baxter's book was seeping into him. He had gone for several hours now and not even thought about how to become more searcher intensive.

Later that morning, Sam found himself at the front door of the Trakowsky home. His finger seemed suddenly too short, too heavy, to reach out and push the pearl button of the doorbell. Inside he could hear the muffled drone of something audio—a radio, a TV, a CD player. He felt sure Frank's widow was at home. He felt sure she must also have been sorting through the whole universe for some logical answer to the great *why-me* questions of life.

*Do pastors have the right to invade the lives of needy people? With caution, yes. Just as a fireman has a right to save a person from a burning building. Urgency is the agency that grants authority to our barging into people's lives. Why then do we back from our calling? Perhaps we spend so much time trying to be professional and nice that we forget urgency plays by another set of rescue rules. We're always out to create a community image that is proper, and herein lies the rub. "We are lured by our own insecurities," writes Eugene Peterson, "into trying to make ourselves better than others, instead of letting God use our gifts in faithfulness to and reliance on him. Faith is a shield against our misconceptions and competitions. Faith knows that our worth is derived from the one to whom we belong, that God's love embraces us and sets us free to be truly ourselves."[73] What we are usually fighting when we make a call on those who haven't invited us is not so much their objection to our being in their world, but the feeling that we might possibly be damaging our image.

†Pastoral care is a world of unbearable pain. However high we lift our spirits in personal or public worship, it is good to remember that many in our congregations come and go from our worship with broken hearts. In some ways this is what is most wrong with public invitations. We ask all those who are shrinking back from life to come forward. But they are refugees from sociability. They want to hide; they do not want to come forward. They want to hide out, so pastors must go to their hiding places. We must come down from our soaring worship and enter the world of unbearable hurt. Rainer Maria Rilke writes:

> I come home from the soaring
> in which I lost myself.
> I was song, and the refrain which is God
> is still roaring in my ears.

> Now I am still
> and plain
> no more words.

> To the others I was like a wind:
> I made them shake.
> I'd gone very far, as far as the angels,
> and high, where light thins into nothing.

> But deep in the darkness is God.[74]

We are called to help the hurting world remember that deep in the darkness is God.

‡In thirty-five years of pastoring, I cannot recall a single instance when a grieving person did not invite me into his circle of woe. It was an honor of which I even yet stand in awe. Therese of Lisieux found that she not only redeemed those she

Sam rang. He felt obscene in doing so. What was he doing here? What would he say when she answered the door? What certifying agency gave him the right to be there?* He earnestly began to pray that she wouldn't be home. God seemed to answer. No one responded. He shuffled on his feet and rang the doorbell again. This time he earnestly prayed that no one would be home. Again it seemed as though God was about to answer his prayer. He felt immensely relieved as he turned to leave. Walking away from the door with a song of deliverance in his heart, he froze. His inner alleluias faded into an "oh, ratz!" The door flew suddenly open. There stood a woman. Her face looked torn by some unimaginable grief. Her eyes were red from being forced to live in a world of unbearable pain.†

"Mrs. Trakowsky? Frances Trakowsky?"

"Yes, I'm Frances Trakowsky," said the woman.

"I'm Sam. I was with Frank the other night just before he died." Sam felt he was blurting out the truth too suddenly, but then again he knew that bad news never improved with keeping. "Frank asked me to give you this," said Sam, extending the photo taken from the truck driver's wallet.

She took the picture, studied it for a moment, and broke into tears. "It was taken last year on Labor Day ... we were fishing at the lake," she managed to say before she broke once again into tears. When she finally recovered from her tears, she turned toward Sam and said, "Won't you come in?"‡

"Thank you, yes," said Sam. He followed her into her small, modest home. It was not a grand place, but it seemed possessed of an unusual warmth. Sam tried not to let his eyes study overlong the eclectic gathering of furniture. Most prominent in the home were two model rigs of eighteen-wheelers. They were beautifully made and must have cost a great deal. They looked like Franklin

helped; she redeemed herself through pastoral care: "One evening not knowing how to tell Jesus how much I loved him and how much I longed for him to be honored and served everywhere, I thought with sadness that not a single act of love ever ascended from the gulfs of hell . . . . It was about this time that our Lord gave me some insight into the souls of children; I spent a lot of time looking after two girls during their mother's illness."[75] In caring for others she came to find out who she was. Teresa of Calcutta experienced the person of Christ every time she engaged in any work of pastoral care.

*The great conundrum in pastoral care is how and when to touch others—particularly the opposite sex. Touching is the final boundary of permission. Yet there is nothing more powerful than the ministry of touch. In my book *The Valiant Papers*, the angel Valiant laments his inability to touch as humans do: "What a blessing is simple skin! What confirmation mortals find in touching each other. Where there is touching men grow secure and lovers delight themselves. Where there is too little touching, frightened children weep at night, and the race grieves."[76] Touch is health, yet its boundaries are formidable, and permission in some form must always be given.

Mint reproductions. One of them was so large it extended for half the length of the coffee table that was its much more cheaply made pedestal. Frances Trakowsky caught Sam's eyes studying the huge models with interest.

"My husband loved trucks," she said. "He always wanted to own his own rig—to go into business on his own . . . but now."

She bit her lip to fight back the tears.

"Mrs. Trakowsky . . ."

"Please call me Frances," she objected.

"Frances," Sam began again, "I was with Frank when he died. He made me promise to bring you the picture. He also asked me to tell you he was sorry for the quarrel."

It was too much. The trucker's wife broke into anguished sobbing. Sam moved nearer to her and reached out to take her hand. It seemed too little. So he moved even closer and put his arm around her shoulder and hugged her briskly.

Even as he did so, he remembered all those seminary counseling courses whose doctrine was never to approach a woman to touch her. "Always care," said his counseling professor, "but only at a distance."* Still it all seemed too remote at the moment, so Sam did what every good preacher does in the act of caring. He touched, pure and chaste from afar, as Don Quixote once said.

When Frances had quit crying, Sam took his former place, somewhat a little more distant from her grieving form.

"Frank asked me to help him pray," said Sam. "He wanted you to know that he recovered all the ground he had lost with God. He came full circle and died in grace."

"Oh, Reverend. I'm so sorry about our quarrel. I would have given anything if we had ended our last moments together in a more civil manner. Please, Reverend, would you help me to pray. I'm so distant from God. I feel so needy."

*The caregiver seems ever godlike to the needy. Again Rainer Maria Rilke says it best for me: "You are the deep innerness of all things."[77] But it is this deep innerness that is so unspeakable. Those who beg the preacher's attention are often asking for God's attention. This is just the way it comes out.

†Baxter seems to go ahead of Sam, beckoning him into ever tighter circles of pastoral care.

‡If there seems an unnatural tug of war between the big church and the little church in this tale, recognize that the mood is both real and widespread. Most pastors of old-line, denominational churches are aware that they are minor players in the wake of the large church trend in America. George Barna confirms this: "The elders of the nation's small churches are just that: elderly, longtime members who have typically served on the governing board for many years. Change of any type comes slowly to these churches. They are proud of their history and see great value in continuing the traditions on which their church was founded. The facility in which they meet, a modern and attractive structure when it was first built many decades ago, now looks tired and worn. The pastor's constant challenge is not only to encourage his dissipating flock but also to imagine creative ways of bringing new life into the church. Such churches represent half of all Protestant churches in the United States."[78]

Sam agreed.

They prayed together a simple, step-by-step prayer, as the trucker's woman came into a new and strong relationship with God.

"Thank you," she said when the prayer was finished. "Oh, Reverend, you will do Frank's funeral service won't you? We weren't church people. We didn't know any other preachers."*

Sam agreed. He promised to "take care of everything." He would call the "Rand Mortuary within the hour." He further promised to get in touch with Mrs. Trakowsky once more by late afternoon.

As Sam started for the door, Frances Trakowsky smiled at him. "Your friend Baxter was right about you," she said.

"Baxter?"

"The English gentleman you sent ahead of you."†

Sam was stunned!

Still he said nothing else except, "Till this afternoon then?"

"Yes, and evermore, thank you, Reverend."

At lunchtime Sam met with Biff Wheeler, who had agreed to leave the lunchtime at the VVSPS to have lunch with his friends. They often met at the Loaves and Fishes Coffee Shop of the Beltway Community Church, a grand coliseum that Father Ambrose liked to call *Our Lady of I-80* mostly because of its gargantuan size.‡

"Hey, PTL!" said Biff, slapping Father Ambrose on the back. "I forgot to ask you guys on Tuesday what you preached on last Sunday."

"It was Ascension Sunday," said Father Ambrose. "I just preached on the incarnate Christ and the gospel imperative. How 'bout you, Sam?"

"Count me about the same. I hit the same lectionary text. I preached on missions, too. How about you Biff?"

*The megachurches have been rich and powerful and as such have in many cases lost interest in anything distant and expensive as mission is. "Christianity is flourishing wonderfully among the poor and persecuted, while it atrophies among the rich and secure."[79] But it is not altogether clear whether the materialism of America's great megachurches is the only culprit in their loss of interest in all things global. "For all their vast wealth, many churches in North America and Europe have far less interest or commitment in the global South than they once had. American mainline churches have dramatically cut back on their budgets for missions. In large measure, this represents a response to charges of cultural imperialism in bygone years, and a guilty sense that there was much injustice to the conventional stereotypes of missionary work."[80] While mainline churches have dropped their interest in global missions, the megachurches never seem to have acquired much of an interest in the subject.

†Marva Dawn relies heavily on Jane Healey's work to describe the dumbed-down church. The church has become increasingly a place of clichés as the members who worship in it have less intelligence to learn and express their faith. Dawn believes that churches lack "patience with the slow, time-consuming hand work by which intellects are woven."[81] Marva Dawn, continuing to rely on Jane Healey, states that earlier in the century fourth-grade public school reading tests were more involved than ninth-grade reading tests from 1988. Naturally, the church is bound to suffer, and her suffering results in a more cliché-driven, less IQ-driven form of learning and worship. Things are so bad here at the first of the new millennium that Os Guinness says, "The more educated now tend to be significantly less religious; those more religious, tend to be significantly less educated. For example, evangelicals are the only religious group in America that exceeds the national average of those not completing the eighth grade or high school. At the same time only 24.2 % of evangelicals achieve some university training, compared with 68% of non-Christians."[82] What this means, practically speaking, is that one's chances of meeting a college-educated person are more than twice as great on the sidewalks of any city than inside the evangelical churches of that city.

‡If Biff seems a bit arrogant, the reader needs to remember that megachurch members usually are exuberant in expressing their identity in terms of the size and importance of their church. "Most people have complimentary things to say about the worship services of their church," says George Barna.[83] But most people like expressing their identity in terms of their heroes, said Ernest Becker in his 1977 Pulitzer laureate book, *The Denial of Death.* Never has there been a day when megachurch pastors have become cultural heroes par excellence.

§Os Guinness may have been a bit severe when he referred to our age as the idiot culture. "Gone are the days when students can rely on the excellence and originality of their writing. The competition of ideas and expression has given way

94

"Missions? Missions?" Biff said it twice, as if the repetition would help him understand.* "Hallelujah! I preached on the 'Winnin' Grin of Winnin' Men!' Did you know that only three percent of the upwardly mobile have any written goals for their lives." Sam felt ashamed he didn't know that. Father Ambrose didn't know it either.

"That's why I gave 'em the old rock 'em, sock 'em, lettin' 'em know that where you go hereafter depends upon what you go after here."

Everything Biff said was laden with clichés, but then that's how Biff saw the world. If there wasn't a cliché to explain any truth, it hadn't been around long enough to be very important, or it was a truth that had been championed by those who were so intellectual they held no place for really clever ways of saying things.† "How did you feel about how well you did in the pulpit?" asked Father Ambrose.

"Well, praise the Lord, course I can't take all the credit, but it was another home run for Jesus! Course that's usually what happens at Beltway Community.‡ Comes from preaching the Book and trusting the Spirit. We have the Word and the Bird, you know! Most people said the sermon just blessed their socks off!"

Father Ambrose smiled. "Better that than their trousers."

The metaphor had suddenly outgrown Biff's ability to understand.

When breakfast was served, Biff offered, "Can I do the little kapow for the breakfast chow?" which was the way any pastor contempo would ask to say the blessing. Both Father Ambrose and Sam agreed that it would be fine. He had blessed their breakfast before. It intrigued Father Ambrose that anyone could talk to God using words and phrases completely borrowed from the evangelical culture.§

to a game of gimmicks in which originality has become zanyness."[84] I recently served on the translation force for a new Bible. I was amazed to discover that virtually all new translations of the Bible are done on an eighth-grade reading level or less. This was amazing to me to know that the King James Version requires a twelfth-grade reading level to understand, and the microwave instructions on a TV dinner requires only a fifth-grade education. Is it any wonder then that the church borrows its language rather than invents it? Creativity suffers in the church just as it does in the culture.

*Do those who involve their reading habits in common titles really awaken their souls to the needs of the world? Can they, therefore, minister to a world they can't see?

†The question is, does Will Willington minister to sixty thousand, or does he just preach to sixty thousand? Kurt R. Schuermann, a Methodist pastor, makes this comment on the subject: "Sometimes I get uneasy around too much talk about church growth. I often think that churches reflect American culture's obsession with size, glamour and even celebrity . . . . Churches seem to want bigger buildings, larger numbers attending, better landscaping, and off-street parking. If 500 in worship is good, then isn't 5,000 in worship ten times better ?. . . It would be interesting to find a church that said 'no' to the addiction to more and bigger. Maybe we could get to a place where we could recognize and appreciate the small and subtle nudges to faithfulness God makes in all congregations."[85] The size of a church does not indicate how well it is doing in ministry.

‡Megachurch giving has proved fairly ineffective: "The size of a church a person attends is related to the giving habits; the smaller the church the less money the typical individual member donates. Adults attending churches of less than 100 gave an average of $488 in 1999; adults attending churches of 100–200 gave a cumulative average of $794; people attending churches of 201 to 999 members gave a mean $1,561, but megachurch giving dropped to $1,462 or less as the church continued to get bigger."[86]
    Still, while megachurches received more money, they were more likely to spend their income on their own needs to the exclusion of missions or other parachurch organizations.

"Lord, bless this food and the hands that prepared it," offered Biff. "And Lord, we pray that you'll hide us behind the cross so that people see only Jesus through us. And Lord, help us to walk the walk so when we talk the talk people won't knock the Rock." Biff's blessing suddenly took a mystical and confessional turn. "Lord, help me never be ashamed of the flame, and to remember that all those times I saw one set of footprints, they were yours. And, Lord, I still think the old violin went too cheap. Amen!"

"Amen!" agreed Sam.

"In nominee Patri, et Filii, et Spiritus Sancti," said Father Ambrose, who seemed to feel it was most important to let God know that one of them knew something to pray they hadn't picked up from the PTL Network.

"Hey, have you guys read *The Neon Yahweh* yet?"*

"No, I'm afraid not," said Father Ambrose.

"Me neither," confessed Sam.

"Well, it's the greatest book since *The Prayer of Jehudi!*" confessed Biff.

"That good?" asked Sam in unbelief.

"Absolutely. This book is changing the way I sort the laundry."†

"Only once or twice," said Ambrose.

"Hey, tonight we're downloading Willington's final simulcast. This is the one where he talks about how to catch up on your searcher intensive index. You need that if you're ever going to see your church really begin to get big and bring in the big bucks.‡ Hey, you guys wanna send some of your people over?"

"Only if you keep 'em," laughed Father Ambrose. "I've got some who need a new church home. They don't much care for the one they've got."

*Biff is both right and wrong in how he perceives the committee theory of pastoral care. George Barna writes, "One of the oddities about American participation is they do not get involved because it is the 'right thing to do.' More often people get involved because they believe they can make a positive difference; they can use their talents and abilities to mutual benefit or because they are responding to an urgent need which they're recruited to address. In many churches these days, none of those criteria are evident, and, consequently, people choose to put their creative energies elsewhere."[87] Biff is right about the fact that people want to be involved, but apparently pastoral care is not one of the areas. In my experience as a pastor, most laypeople do not feel comfortable in hospital or crisis counseling. Or they simply turn from it because they feel it is the work of a specialist more than they are.

†Many of today's megachurch pastors are not seminary graduates and are often critical of what they consider the ineffective methods of seminary-trained pastors. This animosity further aggravates the antipathy between the mainline denominational churches that put an emphasis on hiring seminary-trained pastors and those that don't.

‡One at a time is definitely what Baxter believed: "What a happy thing it would be, if you might live to see the day, that it should be as ordinary for people of all ages to come in course to their ministers for personal advice and help for their salvation, as it is now usual for them to come to the church to hear a sermon or receive the sacrament! Our diligence in this work is the way to bring this about."[88]

§Seventy-five percent of American churches have less than 150 members. Mark Stephens knows this and asks, "Why then are most church resources, books, and conferences designed for the large church, or aimed at the transformation of a small church into a mega-church?

"Conventional wisdom says a large church can offer people what they're looking for. Such wisdom assumes that people are looking for programming choices and more activities. However, research suggests an unchurched person is not looking for that mega-church. He or she desires a much smaller church where people are valued over programs, where connections count more than committees.

"In one denomination churches with a membership of 200 or fewer did a better job of evangelism than did the larger churches. Put another way, the smaller church is able to use fewer members to gain more converts than megachurches—by a large margin."[89]

"I can't attend the simulcast this afternoon," said Sam. "I've got a lot of hospital calls to make. I've got some mighty hurting folks right now," said Sam.

"Hospitals!" Biff was shocked. "I thought you were through with hospitals. Man, turn that over to your hospital visitation committee.* That's what I do. That's why the Lord made laymen, to go see other sick laymen. Hospitals are so unproductive, Sam. You need to be downlinking things. I think it's seminary that gets you educated men all messed up.† That's what I admire about Will Willington of Park Brook. He never went to seminary, and he has the highest searcher intensive index on the East Coast."

The conversation suddenly took a new direction.

"Let me read to you from a little book I recently found." Sam judiciously decided not to tell them the origin of the book or how he had come to have it. Without saying anything further he began to read:

A world of broken heartaches,
Lies neath the bleeding sun.
And though souls die by multitudes
Their healings come by ones.

"Whoa," said Biff, "is he saying what I think he's saying? Is he advocating that busy ministers have the time for one-on-one ministry? It'll never work!‡ Who was this guy?"

"He was a pastor."

"I'll bet he had a little church."

"He believed a church's size was not an indication of its greatness."§

"That's crazy. How else can you measure greatness? Show me a good loser, and I'll show you a loser."

*Leith Anderson says in *Leadership That Works* that most parishioners do not list faithfulness as a key virtue of the pastor. I think he is right on that subject, but it may be an indication of a dumbed-down culture more treasuring the glitzier values of life.

†Perhaps the inner Christ is the last authentication that we have pleased God with our pastoral care. Christ in us reaching to the needy—the Christ beyond us—is the evidence that we have an authentic ministry of pastoral care. Only then can we begin to ask Brennan Manning's great question of self-authentication: "Do I spend my days loving? . . . Does the rhetoric I employ to describe life in the Spirit match the reality of my daily discipleship? Have I grown complacent with what I give because it conceals what I withhold?"[90]

‡Does the style of worship mandate content? While the current worship wars would mandate a big "no" to the question, in actuality, style does mandate content. Biff is right in accusing his Episcopal colleague of a form of worship more common in mainline churches. It does not fit the community church model and, in general, would offer more theological content than other forms. Marva Dawn confesses that she sang in one contemporary worship service the chorus "I Will Celebrate, Sing unto the Lord," a chorus which mentions the word "I" twenty-eight times. She alleges that God is clearly not the subject of the song; the ego-centered worshipper is. On the other hand, Johann Sebastian Bach (1685–1750) said, "God's gift to his sorrowing creature is to give them joy worthy of their destiny."[91]

When I consider Bach's idea that worship should be worthy of our destiny, it makes me want to trade in the ditties of the contemporary church for the excellences of great poets in love with Jesus.

§From 1992 through 1999 Protestant church attendance dropped by 12 percent while the nation's population increased by 10 percent.[92] The bodies experiencing the greatest decline were Methodists, who dropped in population from 12 percent of the population in 1982 to 8 percent in 1995. During the same time the Lutherans dropped from 7 percent to 4 percent, and the Presbyterians dropped from 5 percent to 3 percent.[93]

"Know what else the man said, Biff?" Sam didn't wait for Biff to answer. He turned to Baxter's book and reread to his friends what had so moved him the night before:

God, can I be counted faithful?
This world is such a hurting place.*
So large the bleeding hereabout.
So small my bandages of grace.
Shall I of England fashion Galilee?
Christ shant in Kiddermaster be,
Unless he deigns to live in me.†

"You gotta be reading Baxter," offered Father Ambrose.

"Was he Epicolopian?" asked Biff, badly mangling the name of the denomination.

"Sort of," said Ambrose. "He was a Puritan. And a Puritan was just an Anglican with a prayer life." Sam laughed ever so slightly; Biff didn't get it.

"I thought so," said Biff. "Those guys never could grow churches. They sing too many hymns and don't preach the Bible. What's the matter with you old-line denominationalists? Are you committed to a death wish."‡

"Whoa," said Ambrose. "Our collective Bible readings from all parts of the service last week numbered over 110 verses."

"You can overdo a good thing," offered Biff. "I sure hope you use PowerPoint, or they'll never get through that tangle. Amby, do you have any idea what your searcher intensive index is? Aha! Got you on that one."

"My good man!" said Ambrose stiffly. "Our church was started in the Middle Ages."

"Too bad you never left it," snipped Biff.§

*The Lord is in all our people, even in the ones in which we find it hard to see him. Emma may have been Sam's lifelong nemesis, but she, like all of God's people, contains the same Christ as the pastoral care person who is called to minister to her. "The Lord is in the people with whom we rub shoulders every day, the people whom we think we can read as an open book. Sometimes he's buried there, sometimes he's bound hand and foot there, but he's there. We've been given the gift of faith to detect his presence there, and the Holy Spirit has been poured into our hearts that we may love him there. For the meaning of our religion is love."[94]

†Every true caregiving pastor must face the sin of partisan caring in his calling to care for everyone. Sam is right to feel the need to repent and even more right to ask for forgiveness for an unpleasing attitude toward any member of his flock. "Of the many things which impede our salvation the greatest of all is that when we commit any transgression we do not at once turn back to God and ask forgiveness. Because we feel shame and fear we feel the way back to God is difficult, and that he is angry and ill tempered toward us, and that there is great need of preparation if we wish to approach Him. But the loving-kindness of God utterly banishes this thought from the soul."[95]

Sam could tell the two of them were becoming a bit over-heated. He stood to leave. So did Father Ambrose.

"Hey you fellows, if you have to miss tonight's simulcast, maybe you would like to come to our Right-Behind Concert on Thursday?"

"Not me," said Sam.

"Not me either," said Ambrose. "Ta, ta!"

"Ta, ta!" said Sam laughing.

"Here, there, or in the air," said Biff.

Sam left the Loaves and Fishes and went on to the hospital.

He encountered Emma Johnson in a brand-new way.* She was pallid and her face was drawn. Still, she managed to smile weakly, but Sam could tell she was in a lot of pain.

"I can tell you don't feel good, Emma," Sam offered.

"I didn't know I could feel this badly."

"I know you are to have a biopsy later today."

"I had it this morning. Doctor could tell, I'm in trouble, Sam—deep trouble! It's melanoma, Sam. The doctor says I won't be around much longer."

Sam was stunned. He felt a tiny rush of shame. Shame for all the times he hadn't worked harder at getting along with Emma. There were times when she had made his life hell in the congregation, yet suddenly Sam was reluctant to remember all that.†

"Sam, I know I am too outspoken. I know I used to criticize your sermons too much. But I have to tell you in recent months your sermons are the high point of my week. Still, Sam, I would really appreciate it if you would spend more time with the sick and infirm. We need you too. You know, we who are sick have spiritual needs that only a pastor can help with. I used to believe that the only thing that mattered for a pastor was for him to be a good preacher. But you know what I believe now?"

*John Claypool suggested that the best model for any pulpiteer is Henri Nouwen's *Wounded Healer*. This is to say that the only great preaching that can occur grows out of the pastor's cure of souls. To be wounded is not only to heal; it is to preach with authenticity. Carlyle Marney once said that only when we listen to our people for twenty hours a week do we have the right to preach to them for twenty minutes a week.[96]

Sam shook his head that he didn't.

"Now I believe that only when a pastor is the sermon does he matter much.* You see, Sam, when I look out ahead, all that matters to me is God. When a pastor is a sermon, he will live in the center of his community and love God. Now, Pastor, I know you are friends with that Biff Wheeler, and he might be enticing you to try and grow that same kind of church he has, where the members seem to need less of God to live than the rest of us. I just want to encourage you to remember that the world is full of multitudes of dying people who can only be reached one at a time."

Sam was stunned.

"Let me read you something, Emma," said Sam as he took out Baxter's little black book. Once more he fondled its yellow pages and the spinal stitching that was already beginning to turn loose in some places. Sam read:

> The world of broken masses lies 'neath the bleeding
> suns.
> And though they die by multitudes their healings come
> by ones.

Sam stopped reading.

Emma was dozing. Obviously the anesthetic had not yet worn off.

Sam touched her hand and she blinked awake.

"Emma, I would like to pray for you," said Sam.

"Would you read me the Forty-Sixth Psalm first?" she asked.

Sam nodded and opened his Bible and began to read. When he finished, Emma had nodded off again. He prayed for her while she slept and then walked out of the room.

Sam took the beltway back to the church growth conference he had paid a fortune to enroll in. As he approached Biff's church,

*John Claypool confesses: "Arthur Miller has captured this cultural ideal graphically in the tragic figure of Willy Loman, who was driven all his life to come out the number one man." Willy emerged from the competitive fray murmuring, "I'm number one, I'm number one." Claypool continues: "Although I certainly did not process all of this intellectually, at an exceedingly early age I became what might be classified technically as *Homo Competetus*. The overwhelming drive of my life became 'to make it,' 'to get ahead,' 'to out-achieve all others,' so as to do something about that awful emptiness I sensed at the bottom of my being."[97]

†Perhaps it's worth mentioning that while most of us will never be in the company of a dead English preacher we are constantly surrounded by a great crowd of witnesses who do care about our lives and fortunes and, above all, our ministries. I once sat at a banquet with the late Norman Vincent Peale. I relished the moments with him. I particularly wanted to ask him about a time while attending a big conference in Georgia he thought he saw his long-departed father coming down the aisle singing hymns. I put the questions to him straightforward. "Tell me," I said, "about the time that you thought you saw your long-departed father at a camp meeting." He bristled a bit and then said very sternly, "Thought? Thought? I didn't think I saw him; I actually did see him." The conversation ended, but I was convinced that what his father thought of him had meant a great deal to him and guided him all through his life, even long after his father had entered immortality. Who knows all the ways that the godly dead may speak to us?

it suddenly occurred to him how much it looked like an ancient coliseum. "Spartacus would have been proud, Biff," he said, as he wheeled into a parking place. He wondered if he would ever have a church that large. *Probably not,* he thought. One thing the recent events in his life as a pastor giving care had taught him: he would never again think of himself in competition with the megamen. Competing with other ministers just to outdo them in church size was unworthy of God.* He thought again of Emma and what she said about a pastor loving God and living in the center of his people. He thought about how important it was to be a sermon instead of merely preaching them. He wrangled through his mind the old proverb, *Is a sermon a person preaching good or a good person preaching?*

He managed to get into the late afternoon session just as Will Willington of Newark's Park Brook Community Church stood up to speak. No sooner had he taken his seat when in came Baxter and sat down right beside him. Surprisingly, Father Ambrose was sitting in the row just behind him.

"Here all by yourself?" asked Ambrose, leaning across the pew.

"No, Baxter's here with me," said Sam.†

"Baxter?"

Sam turned toward Baxter and said, "Baxter, I'd like you to meet Father Ambrose."

"Are you all right?" asked Ambrose.

"Sam, old chap, best let it pass!" said Baxter. "He can't see me like you can. Can't hear me, either."

"He can't see you!" Sam sounded animated, maybe even infuriated.

"Sam, are you OK?" Ambrose was most concerned. "I'm coming up there to sit with you, Sam," he said as he made his way forward to Sam's pew and prepared to sit down on Sam's left.

*Baxter wrote there was a sin in pastors not knowing their people: "How many ministers are there in England that know not their own charge, and cannot tell who are the members of it." A pastor was to feel a commitment to each member of his flock that precluded his leaving it for any extended time. Baxter went on to quote the Sixth General Council at Trull, which stated that any minister who left his church for more than three days was to be excommunicated.[98]

†"Is this all thy compassion for lost sinners? Wilt thou do no more to seek and to save them? . . . Shall they die and be in hell before thou wilt speak to them one serious word to prevent it. Shall they there curse thee forever that thou didst no more in time to save them."[99]

"No, don't sit there; you'll sit on Baxter," said Sam with such firmness that Ambrose rose and moved to the open place on his right. Ambrose eyed Sam as he continued whispering to the vacant air on his left side.

"Really, is it all that important that you come to the Successful Pastor's Seminar, Baxter. You're not going to like it. You're not going to agree with it," Sam whispered to—as Ambrose saw it—the empty air on his left side.

Father Ambrose heard nothing for a few seconds, but it seemed to him that Sam must be hearing something because he sat very still with his head tilted toward the vacant place beside him as if he thought he was hearing something. Then Ambrose heard Sam say, "Baxter, I do have your little black book, and I'll give it back to you later tonight if you'll just leave quietly."

But Father Ambrose could tell by the way that Sam kept the conversation going that his imaginary guest was not going to leave. He eventually did appear to sit quietly, for Sam said nothing to him and soon was getting into Will Willington's sermon.

"The first thing that every successful pastor knows," said Willington, "is you've got to delegate all the pastoral care to other care groups in the congregation if you're going to have a big church."

"Wrong!" said Baxter.*

"Shhhh!" said Sam.

"Because leadership is a matter of setting a style and set of priorities within your congregation. A truly successful pastor would delegate his evangelism priorities to the evangelism minister, and try not to win people to Christ yourself."

"Wrong!" said Baxter.†

"Shhh!" said Sam.

"Tending to the spiritual needs of the sick is another boondoggle for the busy times of the pastor's life. Someone else can and

*"Brethren, can you look believingly on your miserable people, and not perceive them calling to you for help? There is not a sinner whose case you should not be so far compassionate, as to be willing to relieve them at a much dearer rate than this comes to. Can you see them as the wounded man by the way? Bring every dying man to the gates of heaven."[100]

should take care of that. Form hospital and long-term compassion groups in the church."

"Wrong! Wrong! Wrong!" said Baxter.*

"It isn't wrong!" said Sam to Baxter.

"I agree with your invisible friend," said Father Ambrose.

"And above all, avoid being too explicit with newcomers. Remember, the searcher intensive church starts gently with people and never brings up complicated things like the cross or heaven or hell or salvation or damnation. Remember this," said Will Willington, "there are four views of hell, and none of us knows which one is right."

"Oh, this bloke's preposterous! Four views of hell," gasped Baxter. "Besides there is and there isn't, what are the other two?"

"Be quiet, Baxter," said Sam, then he leaned in and explained to him in a very quiet voice. "Well, American evangelicals believe that the third form of hell is a modified purgatory, where every body gets the sins singed away so they can go on to heaven . . ."

"Papists! Are they Papists?"

"No, they are evangelicals; they just believe in a limited purgatory."

"What's the fourth view?"

"The fourth view is called annihilationism," answered Sam. "It just means that when we die out of Christ we go poof, and we perish."

"Poof?" answered Baxter. "Is this the poof doctrine of hell?"

"No." Sam was getting too loud now, and several rows of people were looking at him as he tried to answer the thin air above the empty seat beside him. "I told you it's called annihilationism."

Father Ambrose gathered up his black coat and stood.

"Sam, I gotta leave," he said. "But it's my opinion you need to get help."

*Baxter was in favor of preaching both heaven and hell, whether or not his parishioners believed: "What, can you love other men better than yourselves? Can you have pity on them who have not pity on yourselves? Sirs, do you think they will be heartily diligent to save men from hell, that be not heartily persuaded that there is a hell? Or to bring men to heaven, that do not truly believe that there is a heaven?"[101]

"My opinion too," said the man in the row just ahead of Sam.

"But people aren't interested in heaven and hell anymore," said Will Willington. "They want to know how to live a meaningful life. They don't want to know about the cross. It's too bloody, and they don't like thinking about it."

"Wrong!" said Baxter, getting up to leave.* Only Sam knew he was there, and so only Sam knew he was leaving. "About my little black book?" said Baxter.

"Later," said Sam. He smiled as Baxter stood up. He didn't really leave; he just faded out. But Sam was grateful for the fade.

Sam couldn't stay much longer. He decided to skip the rest of the simulcast. But he still had one very important thing to do. He left the church, got in his car, and drove over to Frances Trakowsky's. He told her of the arrangement for the funeral and where he would meet her on the following Friday morning. He would, of course, have to miss the wrap-up session of Will Willington's final Successful Pastor Seminar. Biff Wheeler was sure to be critical of this, but Sam felt that someone had to be with Frances Trakowsky. Her life would never be the same again.

And there was Emma, somehow best when she was at her worst, and worst when she was at her best. Suddenly the sick list loomed up before him. Suddenly he could see that the quality of all we are is better than the quantity of those we count up who happen to come to church because it's too cloudy to go to the lake.

After he had visited with both Frances and Emma, Sam found himself in the easy chair of his den. Home! What a respite for his weariness! He fixed himself a cup of tea and dozed in and out of consciousness. Somewhere in his comings and goings, he was aware enough to see that Baxter had reentered his life. When

*The truth is that churches remain small for the most part. Of the 207,660 evangelical and mainline churches, 170,000 have less than 500 in membership, and 93,000 have less than 200 members.

Sam awoke, Baxter was slumped on the couch opposite the coffee table from Sam.

"Hey, whoa! Baxter! You can't just whisk in and out of my life scaring me like this. What gives?" said Sam. He didn't like the ghost's casual manner, his slinky way of coming in and out of his life.

"Well, old boy, I just couldn't let you get off to sleep without telling you that I was real proud of you today. You ducked out of the simulcast to help those poor people in need. I got the feeling that you are one of the few at the conference who would do that. Everybody there just wants to get bigger churches. I've never seen anything like it."

"Including me. I want to get a bigger church too. I'm tired of being a minor leaguer in a world of major leaguers. I want to matter. I want to have people . . ."

"Gawk at you? Feed your self-importance? Help you build a huge auditorium? Pay off the church mortgage? That's all they are, you know. No artful architecture, no thought given to inspiration. No vaulting transepts. No gilded altars. Just brick boxes with tar-paper roofs. Square rooms with a screen or projector and an amplifier."

"OK! OK!"

"But why do you all compete to build the biggest empty boxes?"

"That's the point. They're not empty. They are filled with people to be gospel fed."

"Yes, and counted!"

"Yes, counted! Listen, Baxter, the only people who don't brag about their numbers in this culture are the people who don't have any numbers to count, or at least have too small a number to count."*

115

*"One of the most heinous and palpable sins is pride. This is a sin that hath too much interest in the best of us, but which is more hateful and inexcusable in us than in other men. Yet it is so prevalent in some of us that it inditeth our discourses, it chooseth our company, it formeth our countenances, it putteth the accent and emphasis on our words. It fills some mens' minds with aspiring desires and designs; it possesseth them with bitter and envious thoughts against those who stand in their light, or who by any means eclipse their glory, or hinder the progress of their reputation."[102]

"Count or boast about?"*

"How else do we measure our success?"

"Success! Is that what you call it—success! Just to get a lot of people in one audience. Nero did that. Bon Jovi does that. When does God get to say what success is? I think I know the Almighty well enough to say that what you have done with your sick members is success."

"I don't care what you say," said Sam. "I want to be big with a big church. I want to be big minded! I want to be Will-Willington-big!"

"Sam, can I tell you that I don't see this as you do? I was not impressed with the bigness of these men—and they are all men. On the other hand, I was impressed with their smallness. They are most parochial really. They don't think globally. I heard no mention of all the people God loves in other parts of the globe. No, dear boy, they are successful on a very local basis. They only reach a narrow strata within their narrow community. They reach neither the poor, nor the rich. They pick a single kind of person, within a narrow window of . . ."

"That's called niche marketing."

"That's called narrow. That's called parochial. That's called little, not big. And the interesting thing about it is that they are all so much alike, championing such minimal differences as they can find. All wanting the same thing, they write books on how unique they are. No, Sam, my boy, you have chosen the best part. Visit the sick, care for the dying, win the lost."

"But I wanna be big!"

"You are big! You know your people. You're not able to just shove them to one side while you build your own reputation. That's what big is—living for other people."

Sam sat silently for a long time.

So did Baxter.

Then in a moment when Sam dozed, Baxter disappeared. Sam felt he wouldn't be seeing him again.

He leaned over and picked up the little black book that was still laying on the coffee table. He thumbed through it and stopped randomly at a passage.

God never calls a man to honor him with loud esteem.
Nor bid him spend his soul on some weak human dream.
God most loves all those who most need him, that's all.
The smallest things grow large when seen as right.
Those things, large labeled, shrink in wiser light.
Large loving bids the world be large.

Sam was ready to add up the lost numbers of his lost esteem. There was much to do. He took the notes of the simulcast and placed it in the back of a file. He had a funeral to preach and hospital calls to make. For now he would enter human need armed only with the all-sufficient Christ. He'd wait to chase his reputation on some later day. "I need you, God," he said. "This world is such a hurting place. How large the bleeding hereabout. How small my bandages of grace."

Notes

[1] Bob Sorrell, with Patrick Springle, *The Next Step* (Cordova, Tenn.: Baxter Press, 2001), 106.

[2] Erwin Raphael McManus, *An Unstoppable Force* (Loveland, Colo.: Group Press, 2001), 31.

[3] Mark Stephenson, "The Big Impact of Small Churches," *Banner* 137:13 (Aug. 2002): 42–43.

[4] Marva Dawn, *Reaching Out without Dumbing Down* (Grand Rapids: Eerdmans, 1995), 62.

[5] Ibid., 69.

[6] George Barna, *The Barna Report* (Jan.-Mar. 1999), 2.

[7] Os Guinness, *Fit Bodies, Fat Minds* (Grand Rapids: Baker, 1994), 89.

[8] Quoted in Os Guinness, *The Call* (Nashville: Word Books, 1998), 35.

[9] George Bernanos, *The Diary of a Country Priest* (New York: Macmillan, 1937), 143.

[10] William Shakespeare, *Two Gentlemen of Verona,* I, ii, 31.

[11] Ed Young and Andy Stanley, *Can We Do That?* (West Monroe, La.: Howard Publishing Co., 2002), 50.

[12] Stephen Macchia, "Becoming a Healthy Church," *Current Thoughts and Trends* 18:8 (Summer 2002), 20.

[13] Dawn, *Reaching Out without Dumbing Down,* 279–80.

[14] Ibid., 62.

[15] Joyce Dinkins, *Christian Thoughts and Trends* 18 (Aug. 2002): 5, 7–8.

[16] Marva Dawn et al., *The Unnecessary Pastor* (Grand Rapids: Eerdmans, 2000), 190.

[17] Chuck D. Pierce and Rebecca Wagner Sytsema, *The Future War of the Church* (Ventura, Calif.: Renew Books, 2001), 180.

[18] McManus, *An Unstoppable Force,* 23.

[19] Ibid., 23–24.

[20] Dawn, *The Unnecessary Pastor,* 5.

[21] Quoted in Leonard Sweet's *Soul Café* (Nashville: Broadman & Holman, 1998), 42.

[22] Ibid., 50.

[23] McManus, *An Unstoppable Force,* 23.

[24] Raniero Cantalamessa, O.F.M. Cap. *The Mystery of Pentecost* (Collegeville, Minn.: The Liturgical Press, 2001), 15.

[25] Quoted in Lawrence Kimbrough's *Words to Die For* (Nashville, Tenn.: Broadman & Holman, 2002), 89.

[26] McManus, *An Unstoppable Force,* 173.

[27] Charles P. Schmitt, *A Heart for God* (Shippensburg, Pa.: Destiny Image Publishers, 1995), 94.

[28] Sweet, *Soul Café,* 51.

[29] Leonard Sweet, *Carpé Mañana* (Grand Rapids, Mich.: Zondervan, 2001), 113.

[30] Dawn, *The Unnecessary Pastor,* 4.

[31] Sweet, *Carpé Mañana,* 87.

[32] William Willimon and Tony Campolo, *The Survival Guide* (West Monroe, La.: Howard Publishing Co., 2002), 54.

[33] Guinness, *Fit Bodies, Fat Minds*, 88–89.

[34] Richard Rohr, *Everything Belongs* (New York: Crossroads Publishing Co. 1999), 33.

[35] Willimon and Campolo, *The Survival Guide*, 79.

[36] From the book jacket of Thomas Howard's *Evangelical Is Not Enough* (Nashville, Tenn.: Thomas Nelson, 1984).

[37] Young and Stanley, *Can We Do That?*

[38] Max Lucado, *Just Like Jesus* (Nashville, Tenn.: Word Books, 1998), 36–37.

[39] Ibid., 127–28.

[40] Young and Stanley, *Can We Do That?*, 143.

[41] *The Barna Report* (Oct. 1999), 6.

[42] John Haggai, *Lead On* (Waco, Tex.: Word Books, 1986), 12.

[43] W. E. Sangster, *The Craft of Sermon Construction* (Aylesbury, Bucks, UK: Pickering and Inglis, 1954), 12.

[44] Warren Bennis, *Why Leaders Can't Lead* (San Francisco: Jossey-Bass, 1992), 83.

[45] Calvin Miller, *The Empowered Leader* (Nashville, Tenn.: Broadman & Holman, 1995), 13.

[46] Young and Stanley, *Can We Do That?*, 170.

[47] McManus, *An Unstoppable Force*, 30.

[48] J. Stephen Muse, *Beside Still Waters* (Macon, Ga.: Smyth and Helwys, 2000), 113.

[49] Ibid., 43.

[50] E. M. Bounds, *With Christ in the School of Prayer* (New Kensington, Pa.: Whittaker House, 1981), 205.

[51] Quoted by Philip Yancey in *Disappointment with God* (Grand Rapids, Mich.: Zondervan, 1998), 174.

[52] Christopher Lasch, *The Culture of Narcissism* (New York: W. W. Norton and Co., 1979), 245.

[53] Dorotheos of Gaza, from *Daily Readings in Orthodox Spirituality* (Springfield, Ill.: Templegate Publishers, 1996), 69.

[54] Walter Brueggemann, *Cadences of Home* (Louisville, Ky.: Westminster-John Knox Press, 1997), 2.

[55] Paul Little, *Affirming the Will of God* (Downer's Grove, Ill.: InterVarsity Press, 2002), 27.

[56] Christian Schwarz, cited by David Daniels, "Growing Churches Naturally," *Current Thoughts and Trends* 18:6 (June 2002): 20.

[57] Mr. Sock and Nathan Dalton, *Right Behind* (Moscow, Idaho: Canon Press, 2001), 46.

[58] Rick Ezell, *Cutting to the Core* (Grand Rapids, Mich.: Kregel, 2001), 14.

[59] Larry Christenson, *Ride the River* (Minneapolis, Minn.: Bethany House, 2000), 143.

[60] John Eldredge, *The Journey of Desire* (Nashville: Thomas Nelson, 2000), 158.

[61] Chip Dodd, *The Voice of the Heart* (Franklin, Tenn.: Sage Hill Books, 2001), 55.

[62] Ibid., 101.

[63] George Barna, *The Second Coming of the Church* (Nashville: Thomas Nelson, 1998), 27.

[64] Richard Baxter, *The Reformed Pastor* (1656; repr. Edinburgh: Banner of Truth Trust, 1954), 88.

[65] Ibid., 90–91.

[66] Guinness, *Fit Bodies, Fat Minds*, 89.
[67] Baxter, *The Reformed Pastor,* 102.
[68] Ibid., 56.
[69] Ibid., 54.
[70] George Hunter, *The Celtic Way of Evangelism* (Nashville: Abingdon, 2000), 121.
[71] Lloyd Rediger, "Terrorism Revisited in Society and Church," *Clergy Journal* 79:5 (March 2002): 13–16, as quoted in *Current Thoughts and Trends* 8:8, Joyce Dinkins, ed. (2002): 7.
[72] Barna, *The Second Coming of the Church*, 29.
[73] Dawn et al., *The Unnecessary Pastor*, 117.
[74] Rainer Maria Rilke, *Rilke's Book of Hours: Love Poems to God* (New York: Riverhead Books, 1996), 83.
[75] Therese of Lisieux, *The Story of a Soul* (New York: Doubleday, 1957), 83.
[76] Calvin Miller, *The Valiant Papers* (Downer's Grove, Ill.: InterVarsity Press, 1976), 84.
[77] Rilke, *Book of Hours,* 119.
[78] Barna, *The Second Coming of the Church,* 16.
[79] Philip Jenkins, *The Next Christendom* (Oxford: Oxford University Press, 2002), 220.
[80] Ibid., 212.
[81] Jane Healey, quoted by Dawn, *Reaching Out without Dumbing Down*, 6.
[82] Guinness, *Fit Bodies, Fat Minds*, 16.
[83] Barna, *The Second Coming of the Church,* 50.
[84] Guinness, *Fit Bodies, Fat Minds,* 69.
[85] Kurt R. Schuermann, *Ministry Is a High Calling, Aim Low* (Louisville, Ky.: Geneva Press), 33–35.
[86] *The Barna Report* (April-June, 2000), 11.
[87] George Barna, *The Index of Leading Spiritual Indicators* (Nashville: Word, 1996), 66.
[88] Baxter, *The Reformed Pastor,* 183.
[89] Mark Stephens, "The big impact of small churches," *Banner* 137:13 (Aug. 2002): 42–43, as quoted in *Current Thoughts and Trends* 181:11, Joyce Dinkins, ed. (Nov. 2002): 13–20.
[90] Brennan Manning, *The Wisdom of Tenderness* (San Francisco: Harper & Row, 2002), 76.
[91] Dawn, *Reaching Out without Dumbing Down*, 108, 57.
[92] *The Barna Report* (Oct.-Dec. 1999), 6.
[93] Barna, *The Index of Leading Spiritual Indicators,* 35.
[94] Manning, *The Wisdom of Tenderness,* 67.
[95] St. Nicholas Cabasilas, as quoted in Peter Bouteneff, ed., *Daily Readings in Orthodox Spirituality* (Springfield, Ill.: Templegate Publishers, 1996), 25.
[96] Taken from John Claypool, *The Preaching Event* (Nashville: Word, 1980), 123.
[97] Ibid., 63–64.
[98] Baxter, *The Reformed Pastor,* 164–65.
[99] Ibid., 17.
[100] Ibid., 197, 102.
[101] Ibid., 81–82.
[102] Ibid., 137.